THE MISSIONARY MYTH

THE MISSIONARY MYTH

—an agnostic view of contemporary missionaries

RICHARD and HELEN EXLEY

LUTTERWORTH PRESS · GUILDFORD AND LONDON

First published 1973

ISBN 0 7188 2026 6

Printed in Great Britain by
Billing & Sons Limited, Guildford and London

Contents

Acknowledgements

Acknowledgement is made to the following publishers:

Lin Yutang, *The Importance of Living*, William Heinemann Ltd, 1938.

Christian Literature Centre Dodoma, *20 Awkward Questions and 20 Frank Answers*.

Stanley Dale, *To Perish for Their Saving*, Victory Press.

Sam Keen, *To a Dancing God*, Fontana, 1970.

Sir Kenneth Grubb, K.C.M.G., *Crypts of Power*, Hodder & Stoughton, 1971.

Publisher's Note

Lutterworth Press have for many years enjoyed close and special links with missionaries—particularly in the field of Christian literature.

This book in no way represents the assessment of the publishers of the modern missionary situation; indeed, there would be areas of considerable disagreement between the authors and ourselves.

Nevertheless, we think this is a remarkable and important book saying something that needs to be considered both by missionaries and their supporters and also by their opponents.

Inevitably, in the time taken to prepare and publish this book, some of the people mentioned have moved on to different types of service.

CHAPTER ONE

Figures of Fun or Walking Saints?

We are agnostics. And this is a book about missionaries. It is an account of some two hundred missionaries we met and interviewed here and during a year's travelling in Africa. It includes Catholics, Bible-thumping fundamentalists and middle-of-the-road liberal Christians. We first attempt to describe them, and then go on to evaluate them from our own standpoint.

This is perhaps one of the most underexposed stories around. The press and television don't cover a great deal of overseas news; they also don't cover much religion. And if they do cover religion, they show mostly hymns on Sunday evenings. Even if writers do see and like missionary work, they are hard pressed to find anyone who will publish. The only time you really catch a glimpse of what missionaries are doing is when the cameras close in on a nine-day wonder like the cholera disaster in Bengal, or the air lift of supplies into beleagured Biafra. The fact that missionaries had been there for years before and remain years after the cameras depart is not news. Occasionally you get a programme showing the fanatics; conflict and eccentricity are good feature stuff. But the majority are never shown despite the fact that most African hospitals are still run by missionary personnel, and that over 15,000 missionary personnel work in Africa alone. Who would guess, for instance, that 50% of all Oxfam's grants are still administered by the churches? Missionaries are still, in large measure, the people on the ground when it comes to aid programmes. After all, what other qualified graduates are going out permanently for a few hundred a year? Who else is prepared to learn a new language and work in unstable political conditions without a hope of a career structure?

What literature there is about the subject is produced by missionaries about missionaries for missionary society members.

With the exception of the Catholics and maybe the Methodists, it is amateurish, which is not a sin, and unreadable, which is. It fails to tell the story as it is. To us, as non-Christians, what we saw was a revelation. The achievements intrigued us by their variety and extent. Christianity aside, this army of people deserve attention. As a group, they characteristically do not spend their lives chasing affluence, a new fridge or a second car. They are free to look at the problems of development and tackle them. Stephen Carr's story, in Chapter 3, is that of a man who walked 600 miles to survey a farm that wasn't his own, turned down a £14,000 a year job, built a gracious home for £140 and lives on £400 a year. Pippa Gaye, in Chapter 8 runs a 50-bed hospital, a three-hour land-rover drive from the nearest town. She is a nurse and there is no doctor. She came back to the UK to learn radiology—a two-year course—in nine days. She learnt land-rover maintenance at the age of 55.

This book will not be a mere recitation of these 'glory stories': there is a lot that we cannot comprehend, a lot that we dislike, a lot that we are glad to have no part in. But we would be less than honest if we did not recount what we saw, and some of this is remarkable, by any standards.

The book arose because we had by accident come across many missionaries in our aid work—with Oxfam and with a South African organization called Kupugani. We had visited 'mission stations' in Zululand and the Transkei and had caught something of the special atmosphere of such places. We should perhaps have known better, but we found ourselves constantly surprised by the scale and complexity of what we saw. It also seemed surprising that a sense of peace prevailed there despite the pressing-in feeling of apartheid.

We went to Canon John Taylor of the Church Missionary Society and said there was a story here, for agnostics as well as Christians perhaps. Bravely, he sent us out with a brief to cover any denomination and write up exactly what we wanted to say, warts and all. This material was produced as the report *In Search of the Missionary*, Highway Press, 25p. Some of the material in that report appears in Chapters 3, 4, 6 and 12. Because of the response to that report we decided to write this book. We then visited other countries in Africa, and spent three or four months in research back in Britain followed by a month in India.

Before we first left for Africa we discovered that most people regarded missionaries as irrelevant, although the subject was always good for a joke. Sometimes there were hoots of laughter; more often polite interest: 'Oh really, I didn't realize they were still around.' Left-wing friends and Third World First supporters were often hostile, viewing missionaries as neo-imperialist busy-bodies carrying on long after the white man should have left. Even within church circles, the image was thirty or forty years behind the reality.

To outsiders, missionaries are vaguely something left over from another era, smacking of baggy pants and khaki topees. The word itself says as much. In the Pocket Oxford Dictionary, 'missionary' is defined as one who is 'concerned with converting the heathen', and even the most ardent Empire Loyalist must be given to wondering who the heathen are these days. The agglomerate image we built up as we first looked at the subject was something along the following lines: Missionaries went out in Victorian times; they preached to the savages under the shade of a tree or umbrella, covered up breasts and stopped any sexual non-senses, drums or dancing, and got the converts together in neat little thatched hut schools; then, as commerce and Empire proceeded apace, they blossomed forth to become the pillar behind the establishment, supporting all that morally upheld the Queen and the Colonial Office. From jungle bashing heroes of the Livingstone era to the escapist puritanism of the 'thirties, missionaries were a peculiarly English joke (that they were not of course all English is irrelevant) that gave rise to endless cartoons in magazines as diverse as *Punch* and *Titbits*, *Playboy* and the *Daily Mirror*. That the cartoons centred around the cooking pot and nudity is perhaps no accident; most humour is based on people's weaknesses. And the public intuitively grasped that missionaries were usually blind to the resistance of the cultures they were invading. If they ended in the cooking pot, or were—later—thrown out with the end of Empire, they had, after all, asked for it.

But humour, of course, is not only created around those who are vaguely eccentric, pompous or earnest: we also make fun of those who challenge too brazenly our deeper feelings. Whether the subject is nuclear disarmament, environmental doom or missionaries, close examination is uncomfortable. At a time when almost everything is measured in money terms, when even rugged mountains are seen in terms of the tourist revenue or metals to exploit, it doesn't do to take too seriously the unexplained phenomena of qualified young people giving up their lives to go to less comfortable lands at rates of pay that would make a dustman laugh.

So the image remains a myth, and like all good myths it contains its share of truth. The myth can also be exaggerated. Some people do realize that missionaries have moved on a bit from the topeed hat stage. But they still have no new image to replace the old one. They are unaware that ecumenical work has started in many places, that at the start of this century many societies were training local priests and bishops, that the move to independence itself was hastened by the educational work of the missionaries, and that many of today's leaders are mission educated and still Christians: Nyerere, Kaunda and Banda spring to mind.

Both of us shared a few of these preconceptions. We had a mental picture, for instance, of missionaries as middle aged. It came as a considerable surprise to find most of them were our contemporaries. One of the older missionaries put it this way: 'When I go home and address church meetings people say to me "How young you are." In fact I'm forty-three and one of the oldest missionaries in Uganda. But for every meeting I can address there are probably five conducted by kind and well-meaning old ladies who have retired from missionary work and still talk about "When I was in Poona in 1910 . . .".' Again, I suppose we expected most missionaries to be clerics, and fairly formal at that. In practice we only saw one dog-collar outside a church service on the whole trip. It was removed within minutes in favour of a bright African Kitenga shirt. Most of those we met were dressed with complete informality, and were more likely to have dirty knees or grease from their vehicles than to be wearing a suit.

We were surprised, too, at the comparative lack of proselytization. Helen was more than a little apprehensive of being got at by the 'moralistic' people she was going to meet. Evangelization still goes on, but in the overwhelming number of cases, this was in the hands of the locals. Most people we met were doctors, teachers, nurses, or members of professions needed by newly developing countries: agriculturists, engineers, accountants. There

was a willingness to talk about their faith, and plenty of evidence
that this was primarily why they were there. But there was no
attempt to convert us, except in one case where we had asked
for it. One girl expressed this forcibly: 'I'd rather die than go
bible thumping. I'm just no good at it.' Others were content to
see their witness as a quiet thing, caught rather than taught.
There was very little evidence of aggressive Christianity, except
in the African churches themselves which had picked this up
from the earlier missionary patriarchs.,

Many missionaries were themselves embarrassed by the label
'I'd like to get rid of the word, it's so totally misunderstood,' one
of them told us. 'If you wrote me up as a missionary it would
work against the whole aim of what I'm doing,' said another.
You soon realize, in fact, that in church circles the word is as
loaded as 'democracy' or 'communism' is in politics. Missionary
is a word that is overworked and has to describe too many things.
When describing the early pioneers who *did* tramp through jungle
and swamp, it has a clear meaning: everyone is tuned in when
you talk in these terms. But today, when the missionary is in
almost all cases no longer in charge, no longer the big white boss,
it has almost totally changed its meaning. Missionaries can no
longer go and do their own thing, with a convenient crowd of
illiterate natives collected round to listen. They usually have to
be invited, they go out to serve under African leaders, and they
go out with skills which those leaders desire—hence the switch
to agriculture and other disciplines.

The situation in the last twenty years has completely altered
and it is perhaps not surprising that the public here has not kept
pace with the breadth of this change. Missionaries have been
stripped of all power. They have moved from the centre of the
stage to the position of servants, and this has ushered in the
profoundest psychological changes. Except in remoter areas such
as Zaire (Congo), the harsh authoritarianism of an earlier era of
fundamentalists or of conservative Catholics is just not acceptable.
People can be persuaded, they can no longer be compelled; this
too brings a change in the kind of man who wants to go to
Africa.

We found ourselves in most cases reasonably at ease in missionary company, barring one or two memorable exceptions.
The people we met were not the awesome, fierce looking

characters that stared out at us from the early missionary annals we had studied. They were more noticeable for their ordinariness than their eccentricity. They were often the sort of people you would expect to be running a library or teaching in a school back home; unexceptionable with no profound charisma. They were apart in one marked respect, and that was their concept of service and stubborn loyalty to their ideals. Their sense of hard work and dedication put them obviously apart; one also suspected that the huge needs they faced drew forth the best in them.

If the myth is complex, and the word missionary itself is loaded, we will try in this book to look at the reality of what these people, whatever they are called, are doing. We will try to see if they really are human, whether they are relevant in post-independence Africa and Asia, and whether their medical and educational work stands scrutiny.

The book will not be an apologia for Christian missions. We were agnostic when we set out on the assignment; we remain agnostic when it is finished. We hope this fact alone will enable the facts to come across—the sad truth remains that no one really believes advertising, whether it's Hoover selling their products or the Church telling its story. We hope that the absence of an axe to grind will enable non-Christians as well as Christians to gain as fresh and up-to-date a picture of the subject as possible.

CHAPTER TWO

The Authors

We do not pretend total objectivity; in a loaded subject this is probably impossible. Missionaries writing this book would have their biases, and so do we. Our inclinations would naturally be towards the more liberal churches; we feel less at ease with the intolerant or judging. We often found it difficult to have any meaningful dialogue with those who had absolutist views, and this is a bit hard on Christians because in a sense, theirs is an absolutist religion. In general we found ourselves with more in common with those whom the orthodox may dismiss as 'unsound' or 'sub-Christian'. We were much more inclined to look for the effect that Christianity had had in peoples' lives than in the particular brand of theology they subscribed to.

As our own subjective attitudes obviously colour all that follows, it seems only fair to give readers, at the start of the book, a brief biographical glimpse of our backgrounds.

We are both writers, a husband and wife team. Richard is thirty-seven, Helen is thirty. We have two small children of seven and six, and we have worked together almost since the day we met. Richard spent seven years with Oxfam in his early twenties, ending up in charge of their national publicity and doing a fair amount of travelling to developing countries. Although now an agnostic, he is in some ways a reluctant one: a God would be more comfortable. He comes of a strongly Christian background in the liberal tradition, and was at one time a candidate for Holy Orders. Helen was brought up in South Africa, on the other hand, and underwent the worst kind of public school Christianity, followed by a fiercely rational university course in logopaedics and psychology.

Throughout our lives together, we have worked for what might broadly be described as humanitarian organizations. We first lived in South Africa, where we worked for Kupugani, an organization which bought up surpluses of oranges, apples, milk and other agricultural products together with protein foods, milk powder, peanut butter and meat and sold them at cost in the African townships and reserves. We then worked together on Union Artists, an organization originally founded by Trevor Huddleston in Sophiatown; we organized the Independence entertainment for Lesotho, and various African shows that toured South Africa. Richard was General Manager of both organizations. In 1968, with Leonard Cheshire, we launched *Help* magazine in an attempt to give more publicity to the kind of issues in which we were interested. We have stayed in this kind of social journalism and writing ever since, trying both to bring up a family and stay working together as a couple, a combination that is not always easy.

Most of the chapters of the book are written by Richard; most of the research has been done by Helen, together with all the editing. In general we have seen eye-to-eye on our conclusions and reflections, and so have made liberal use of the plural 'we'. But as our religious backgrounds have been quite different, we have felt it worth while to say a few words about each, separately. Let us begin, therefore, with Helen.

*   *   *

I didn't come from a particularly religious family, but I was sent to a diocesan boarding school in South Africa which was high Anglican and very strict.

I hit it at a particularly bad patch when we had a battle-axe of a headmistress. She told us at Assembly on her first morning that she had come out to Africa to 'dispel the mists of ignorance'. We were more than a bit insulted. She then piled on insult to injury by saying how surprised she was to see all the books we carried around, as though she expected us to be in darkest Africa.

Having discovered that we were modern, she proceeded to ban our innocent Valentines, ration our school dances, and read sex into everything we did. I think we were perfectly normal adolescents.

Apart from a puritanical and judging headmistress, we also

had to go to chapel twice a day. Everyone was confirmed in the same form at the same time, and three times a term there was compulsory communion (which is a contradiction in terms if anything is). I think most of the girls were confirmed just because it was the done thing.

I went through a stage for six months in which I was intensely interested in religion and queried everything about it. But my questions upset the parson who was our catechist. I remember him in one class saying how important baptism was, because once you were baptized a Christian you were always a Christian, even if you subsequently became a Muslim. It followed, he said, that we should be sure to baptize our children as soon as possible. My young mind rebelled at the unfairness of this. 'Surely if you're going to be Christian for ever', I asked, 'and if its so irreversible, shouldn't people wait until they can judge for themselves, until they were fourteen, say?' He looked at me, and said stonily 'Don't you trust your mother and father?' After which I sat down and stayed down.

It was perhaps a pity from a religious point of view that I ran into this parson at this stage, because since then I have never met someone quite so dour and judgemental. Or perhaps it's just that they're more polite to me because I'm older and a journalist. He killed anything that could have grown in an enquiring mind. If I had met John Taylor or his like at this stage I still may have not become a Christian, but I wouldn't have had quite the anti-reaction this man gave me.

Nevertheless, I persisted. I read the Bible avidly. I adored the character of Jesus, and what I interpreted this to be then has had the most profound effect on me since. But I refused to sing Amen to the hymns. I didn't refuse aloud. I just quietly shut my mouth. When the creed came and we all had to face the altar. I used to miss out the bits about the Holy Ghost. I just baulked at everything metaphysical.

When my confirmation day came I remember vividly kneeling in front of the Bishop. He put his hands on my head. I don't know what I expected. Perhaps a sort of Holy Spirit, something earth-shattering. I expected to go dizzy or something and have some deep religious experience. For a moment I thought it might have started. But nothing happened. Just nothing. I was terribly disappointed. And I am afraid nothing has ever happened since,

B

although over the years I've gradually come to the position where I'm glad nothing did happen.

In retrospect, what was absolutely classic on that day was an incident involving my mother. After the confirmation, she was called in to see my housemistress, the scripture teacher and a fanatical all-devouring Christian. My Mom knew she'd done something wrong and went in with quaking knees—she said afterwards that she felt just like a little schoolgirl. The housemistress wanted to know why she hadn't been praying like everyone else. She had gone down on her knees, *but she had kept her head up.* Why? My Mom apologized and explained timorously that she was Congregationalist. Afterwards the indignity of the situation suddenly struck her. 'How on earth did *she* know unless *she* was peeping as well!' Mom exploded.

People may dismiss these stories of my school-day religion: 'Oh well, it's not really like that today.' But I'm not that old, and these attitudes are still around, even if they are muted in the presence of people who stand up for themselves. Certainly, as we will explain later, I found just these attitudes reflected in the paternalist attitudes of some of the missionaries we met on our travels, especially exaggerated with a captive or primitive audience.

Although it was years later, these early experiences coloured a lot of my first impressions on the trip we describe in this book. When I first moved in the company of missionaries I felt very much the little schoolgirl. I let my hems down, and had to watch myself for being too noisy, outgoing or swearing—to the extent that I got embarrassed if my fingernails were dirty. This was, of course, overreaction in 90% of cases, as I came to learn: many of the people we met are now among our close friends. But if 90% are accepting, one still can't overestimate the effect that a few tight-up haridans had on me—and still do on the people of Africa today.

When I left school, and went on to university, I faced a totally different environment. I joined a very hard-boiled, rational four-year course in logopaedics and experimental psychology. I developed a total distrust of anything metaphysical. To me, religious people were just in a semi-hypnotic state, inventing a God who satisfied their own psychological and emotional needs.

For years after that I did not meet many religious people, until my editorship of *Help*, which was about social issues. I then found

I was very close to a lot of church people as long as they kept off the subject of God, which honestly embarrassed me. I felt strongly about race relations, justice, poverty and non-violence, and when I found these qualities in Christians I warmed to them. But if they were talking about some issue and suddenly went off at a tangent to talk about the 'Holy Spirit', the 'Trinity' and 'the Lord has blessed this work', I just put what they said in mental brackets. Religion doesn't mean much to me; I really don't feel the need of a 'God-box', despite talking to the small hours and becoming close friends with many Christians. I wouldn't have called myself anti-religious at any stage. It wasn't a crusade with me and I never attacked people in the Church. I just kept clear of it.

On most issues I think you would have called me a humanitarian. Throughout university I questioned the racialism of South Africa, especially the affluence of the northern suburbs of Johannesburg. I started to wear no make-up, to find a lot in common with intellectuals, artists and journalists.

I kept finding myself involved in helping people, organizing multi-racial work camps or volunteering for Kupugani, which distributed protein foodstuffs to Africans in the townships and reserves. This was where I met my husband; I'd been working as a volunteer for some time when he employed me.

From then on I was busy having babies and trying to keep some independence. I have always helped Richard with his work, and when he and Leonard Cheshire started the magazine *Help* and couldn't get an editor, I stepped in for the first issue. About a year later I was beginning to be an editor.

Today I suppose you would describe me as a liberal with a small l, a fairly independent woman without being Woman's Lib; I loathe routine and housework—yet will spend ages cooking an important meal or doing flowers. One *duty* I do enjoy is looking after my kids who are noisy and fun. My great interest is overseas aid, and this is not an intellectual thing, it's a guts thing. I love Africa, I love the laughter and culture of the people. The visit to India opened up a whole world of interests to me. In this way the aid side of missionaries is very close to me, and opens up an immediate sense of communication with most of them.

* * *

This is Richard's story:

My background to Christianity was quite different from Helen's. From a very young age, Christianity was associated with people I respected. My mother kneeled every night to say her prayers, and her beliefs somehow saw her through the storms and tragedies of her life. To me, at Sunday school, all the stories seemed to be about the goodies winning out in the end over the baddies. It was a philosophy that appealed to an early idealism.

When I donned long trousers, and went off each Sunday morning to church on my own, it was to the largest parish church built in England since the Reformation, St. George's, Stockport. Here the church was crowded, sometimes two thousand or more at a big service. A crowded church in the industrial north was a tribute to a remarkable man. Week after week Wilfred Garlick set out a kind of Christianity that I would find impossible to fault to this day. He exuded a kind of liberal hopefulness that brought out the best in people. He preached an utter honesty in money and taxation to his middle-class audience. He preached for faithfulness in marriage and against pre-marital sex, and yet could hold an audience of teenagers with his bluntness.

'Don't worry about masturbation. You'll stop it when you marry. Sex in marriage is like oil in a motor-car. You can't run on oil. But try running without it.'

He preached a crusade against poverty, and had lived this out in his own life, spending years in the slums of Ancoats.

'I remember returning home late one night and seeing the whole road moving. It was a vast army of rats, I was told by the M.o.H. next day, moving from sewer to sewer. I remember being called out another night to a baby which had had half its face eaten away by rats.'

Fight the good fight, in such a context, meant something. When I decided the time had come to be confirmed, I attended confirmation classes conducted by the Vicar, and because these were conducted in an atmosphere of persuasive reason, I was persuaded.

'Christ said he was the Son of God. This was an outrageous claim. He must therefore have been what he said, or a madman. Does he seem like a madman?' It was mainly stock Christian apologetics, but coming from a man I trusted it was completely convincing.

From then on my religious life took a deeper turn. I really felt, as I knelt at the communion rail, that Christ in some mystical sense really existed, and that if I drove all sense of self from me I could be in tune with this mystical force. I was greatly drawn to a kind of self-emptying confessional kind of Christianity. I wanted to serve and serve utterly. Christianity, for me, was a deeply emotional experience at this time. To what extent it was bound up with sex and puberty, I don't know.

As I look back on those teenage years I realize that you can't come through this kind of upbringing without it being very formative. I went to church at least twice a week, sometimes four or five times. I went to early morning services on a Wednesday, to seven o'clock Sunday communion, to morning service, to evensong. And after youth fellowship on a Sunday evening—anything from a missionary film show to climbing in the Hebrides—there was prayers or the office of Compline.

You became steeped in Christian thinking. Every hymn, every anthem, every sermon was trying to guide you along a path, in a Pilgrims Progress sort of way. And if it caught you—as it caught me—it swept you up into a feeling that life had an absolute purpose, that there was clear right and wrong, that the job of your life was to jump in and fight alongside the saints. It was only years later that I hit the things that ordinary pagans take for granted in adolescence—the sham of British society, the pointlessness of the rat race, feelings of rebellion at the futility of life. These were unknown to me.

At about sixteen I decided to become a priest. I went along to a conference on the subject for sixth formers at Birkenhead, where I had my first and last religious dream. It was utterly convincing and devastating. After this I am not one to scoff at religious experience. Later, at another conference, I was accepted as a candidate for Holy Orders. It all seemed wonderful. I loved the quietness, the reverence of the chapels, the sense of dedication, putting your own wishes last.

From this point onwards, the drift from religion began. It started with small things 'This business of Christ descending into Hell, Vicar, I just don't believe it.'

'Ah, well, it doesn't really mean that, it means something else.' One by one I began to question the basic tenets, and the more I questioned, the more I doubted. I brushed up with the authoritarianism of the Church for the first time. I was having tea with the Bishop of Chester, who was not noted for his pacifist views. I was telling him I was a conscientious objector, and intended to apply for unconditional exemption from National Service. I refused to do alternative service in forestry as a sop. I was 100% against military service or any of its ancillaries. 'I want you to do alternative service', the Bishop insisted. I was adamant. 'Would you defy your Bishop?'

'Yes, if he was unreasonable.' There was an awkward silence and an awkward parting.

To become a priest in those days it was desirable to have a degree. 'Don't take divinity.' Wilfred Garlick warned, 'there's a good course in economics and politics at Manchester. Take that. You'll find it much more interesting, and it will give you a useful background.' He was right, but it took me bit by bit away from the Church. I became involved in Bevanite politics, selling *Tribune* on the steps of the university.

When I left university I floundered. I knew by then that the Church was not for me. But what? I knew I wanted to serve people in need, but how? There was no VSO then, or anything like it. So one day I got on my bicycle and cycled round to every hospital within ten miles of home looking for a job. I got one as a ward orderly in a TB sanatorium. Most of the job was serving breakfasts, making beds and emptying bed pans. But it was a base from which to cast around. I wrote off to the World Health Organization, UNICEF, everyone I could think of, asking if they could use someone in a need situation. I got a reply from Oxfam, saying they could offer little abroad, but if I was willing to push a bicycle round the villages of Oxfordshire, I could join them. I leapt at the chance.

I worked for Oxfam for seven years, and in the course of this time travelled a lot overseas. Inevitably I bumped into a fair number of missionaries who make up the stuff of this book. At twenty-four I became Publicity Officer.

During my twenties I gradually drifted further and further from orthodox Christianity. For a time I went to the Quakers because I was attracted by their pacifism and concepts of service. But in the end I failed to join them because I felt I was by then a thinly disguised humanist, and it would be wrong formally to join a society if I did not really subscribe to the central beliefs.

The interesting thing to me in retrospect is the enormous impetus to service that a daily diet of practising Christianity gave. Long after I had formally ceased to be a Christian (whenever that occurred) the thought processes that had moulded me from sixteen to nineteen still provided the impetus. Wilfred Garlick once said to me that the practice of Christianity 'stored up a spiritual capital that could be drawn on in times of adversity.'

When we subsequently met up with a lot of missionaries I was very struck by the fact that their daily habits stored up this same kind of capital. By putting their faces to a particular direction, even if they were quite ordinary sort of people, they became greater for it.

As I drifted further and further from orthodox Christianity in my late twenties, I became aware of much more positive reasons for rejecting Christianity. Before, my rejection had been of a negative kind: I could not believe the miracles, I could not believe the doctrine of the Atonement and so forth. Now, I positively wanted another kind of life. I saw how dreadfully divisive Christianity could be in its stark division into good and evil. More and more of life seemed to be about shades of meaning rather than absolutes. I saw just how much damage the Church had done through its teaching on sex. Most important of all, the Church seemed to have almost nothing to say about the poetry of life. You were always living for tomorrow, for some day when the great battle was won. The idea dawned on me with growing force that life was for here and now. It was beautiful this minute, and the Church seemed to have nothing to say about positive living. There was lots about how you were bound to be a miserable sinner, lots indeed that implied that that is all you can be in this vale of tears. I found the whole thing increasingly gloomy.

I think the film *Zorba* was a watershed for me. Suddenly I saw that the wonder of humanity lay in its poetry, its dance, its art, its sin, its going out and embracing of life. A religion which tried to hold this back was not merely negative, it was pernicious, and I was glad to be free of the thought shackles it imposed. I remember returning to Britain from South Africa in 1967. Although I was opposed to the regime in South Africa in just about every way, I had insidiously imbibed attitudes which I had to carefully discard. So with Christianity. As I move in circles today, and see films like *Midnight Cowboy* I realize that Christianity has laid a stultifying hand on the mind of man. It has its glories, its wonderful sense of love and service, its turning the other cheek. But this is only a part of life, if an overlooked and underlived part.

I once remember asking a group sitting round the Oxfam lunch table: 'What are we going to do when there are no more hungry people in the world: how will life have meaning?' I suggest that only someone brought up in a Christian tradition could think like that. You have to have sinners to have a reason for saving people. It seems a negative life style to me.

I think this extract from the Chinese philosopher of the 'thirties, Lin Yutang, sums up my feeling:

> It is strange that this problem of happiness, which is the great question occupying the minds of all pagan philosophers, has been entirely neglected by Christian thinkers. The great question that bothers theological minds is not human happiness, but human salvation—a tragic word. . . The question of living is forgotten in the question of getting away from this world. Why should man bother himself so much about salvation, unless he has a feeling of being doomed? Theological minds are so much preoccupied with salvation, and so little with happiness, that all they can tell us about the future is that there will be a vague heaven, and when questioned about what we are going to do there and how we are going to be happy in heaven, they have only ideas of the vaguest sort, such as singing hymns and wearing white robes. Mohammed at least painted a picture of future happiness with rich wine and juicy fruits and black-haired, big-eyed, passionate maidens that we lay-men can understand. . .
>
> Are we going to strive and endeavour in heaven, as I am sure the believers in progress and endeavour must assume? But how can we strive and make progress when we are already perfect? Or are we merely going to loaf and do nothing and not worry? In that case, would it not be better for us to learn to loaf while on this earth as a preparation for our eternal life?

*   *   *

These potted and perhaps superficial biographies bear upon the reactions we relate later. We have tried to be ourselves and to give honest reactions rather than to hold back our thoughts and present a more intellectual—and probably more fair—evaluation. We do not pretend to be experts; we have simply told a story as it seemed to us.

In other words, we have not attempted to produce a balanced

study. We have not toned down our first reactions, even when these were sweeping. We have tried to tell the story as it seemed to a couple of ignorant outsiders. For instance, the 'goodness' and 'judging' that we felt at first in missionary company, we no longer notice. But our first reactions were real and therefore valid.

Our main aim has been to give an overall impression of missionaries for they have a story worth telling. But they do have a tremendous communications problem. On a purely practical level, overseas countries are changing very rapidly and development theories are very complicated. There are so many countries to communicate about; there is a tremendous knowledge gap in reaching the public.

Secondly, they inherit their own religious language and with it, religious thought patterns. To a complete outsider, tuning into a religious church service on Sunday is rather like looking in on some strange ritual or mumbo-jumbo. When religious people talk about the 'Holy Spirit' or 'being born again' or 'giving witness', this does nothing to help.

Finally, missionaries have to communicate subtle knowledge they have picked up over years of experience in a strange country. They have to try to communicate to someone who has never travelled, what life is like, what poverty is like. So many of them reject the affluence they see when they come back to Britain. It is one thing for them to feel this but it is another thing to persuade Aunt Mary or a conservative church group that what they see so blindingly is right. It is also one thing to spend years growing to love and respect Indians, to grow to love a few of them and not feel that they are in any way different. It is another thing to communicate this knowledge to a family who fear and misinterpret the strange people next door who cook smelly curries.

We have simply travelled around and tried to describe what we saw and felt. At least this should do something to close the gap.

CHAPTER THREE

The Last of the Bundu Bashers ·

First impressions of a country are usually memorable, and Uganda is no exception. We arrived just before the Amin era. You sweep in on a modern jet over the vast expanse of Lake Victoria, and to all the world it looks as though you are coming down into the lake itself as the wheels touch the thin strip of lakeside runway. You walk out of the air-conditioned craft to the blistering humid heat of the tarmac. Then you drive the 15 miles to the capital through luxuriant tropical vegetation; banana trees, palms, hibiscus, small patches of 6-foot maize. And in that 15 miles you see a microcosm of Africa. The road is crowded with cars from clapped out bangers to occasional ministerial Bentleys; the roadside smallholdings jostle for their subsistence living. The odd chicken scratches away; pigs root for delicacies. The occasional roadside stall dustily shouts its way into the present admass age, with Coca Cola and Sunlight soap emblazonments. Nearer the capital this subtly changes. Well built modern villas begin to dot the highway as those who have made it buy up land around the city. We saw a hundred cars with Ugandan drivers before we saw the first car driven by a white man.

The place we were heading for, the missionary guest house, conjured up almost everything missionaries have been. Set amidst a blaze of bougainvillaea and hibiscus and surrounded by lawns, it lay resplendent in a faded glory up on Namirembe Hill. There were flagstone floors and tall cool rooms, and wooden verandas on stilts surrounded by mosquito netting, and quietly padding, white clad servants. It was not by any stretch of the imagination lush, but it was comfortable and simple, a welcome place to rest after travel.

You could imagine it must have been next to heaven when it was built at the turn of the century and the early pioneers came

in from trudging up country. Now it had the slightly faded air
of bygone middle-class thrift.

Namirembe Hill—guest house and all—is in fact something of
a missionary enclave within a city. Perched above the lights of
Kampala, it comprises a hospital, a church bookshop, a guest
house, a good many missionary bungalows for doctors and dig-
nitaries, the offices of the Secretary and Treasurer of the Church
of Uganda, and above them all the cathedral, a vast great sand-
stone edifice in its gothic majesty, complete with war memorials
to the (British) dead from the two European wars.

In religious circles, Kampala and its hills are almost as famous
as Rome and its hills. Perhaps not without reason. The Roman
Church occupies the opposite hill, Rubaga. It, too, has a cathedral
on top. It, too, has a cluster of administrative buildings, a social
centre, a hospital and an educational complex. Although all is
sweet and light now, the two citadels are a living memorial to
the divided and murky past in which the kingdom of Buganda
fell if the king backed the wrong church at the wrong time.
Missionary history is not all sweetness and light.

*   *   *

The man we had come to see, Stephen Carr, is something of a
legend in missionary circles, and it was with some enthusiasm
that we looked forward to leaving Kampala to motor to his new
plantation at Hoima in Western Uganda.

It is only when you motor through a country like Uganda that
you become aware of the incredible distances that have to be
traversed. Mile after mile of endless primitive agriculture, bush
huts and small clusters of villages are interspersed with fast
modern roads, which are a surprise to the visitor.

The sort of incident we went through on the way out to the
Carr's gave us a first flickering insight into the problems of any
Westerner living in a contemporary African situation. We had
gone about a hundred miles and were stopped by a police road
block. Uganda had been through one of Africa's periodic near-
revolutions. The police were reputedly tough, and several people
had been shot at road blocks the previous week. The police were
polite enough to begin with. Then they asked Richard to open
the bonnet of the car. At this point in time, Richard realized,

with horror, that he had no clue whatsoever how to open the bonnet of our hired car.

'I can't,' he said, 'I don't know how to.'

'Open it,' the soldier said, banging it with his rifle.

Richard felt cold sweat. He pushed and pulled and tugged with everything he knew, until with a sigh of relief, it pinged open. The tension went and the soldiers waved us on our way. Then the car wouldn't start, and for fifteen minutes we attempted to get the car going under the cold stare of the soldiers.

There is a delightful sense of the explorer still to be had in Africa. First you leave the tar road, then you leave the last town, then you turn off on to the minor dirt road, then you turn off on the dirt track; all the while wondering if you have taken the right turn, or whether you are going farther and farther into who knows what. Each mile sees more dense bush—more elephant grass. When you stop the car to listen to the myriad sounds of Africa's bush your mind runs a riot of imagination.

And then you are there. In this case to a settlement of thatched houses set on a hillside, a few hundred feet above a plain. A vast area of beautifully cut lawn, and a drive lined both sides with flowers and flowering grasses. It's an oasis kind of feeling as you come to these few acres of greenery, of flowers, amidst the hundreds of square miles of wilderness that you have driven through.

We had come to meet the Carrs and to hear their story. Stephen Carr is something of an *enfant terrible* among missionaries. One of his colleagues had, in the same breath, called him 'absolutely unsquashable, disgustingly self-confident', and then admitted that his work was one of the two finest examples of missionary work he had seen in thirty years in Africa. We wanted to know more.

His wife, Anne, came across the lawns to meet us, and we were straight away struck by the calm gracefulness of the house as a refuge from the blistering heat. We settled down to cool lemonade, and waited for Stephen.

He came up a few minutes later, looking anything but the image of a missionary. He was wearing old and battered plimsolls, and a sort of scarecrow's cowboy hat, his knees and clothes were filthy, and he was obviously tired. He had been through an exhausting morning building a 60-foot girder bridge over a river.

Stephen had been in South America as a child when the 1939 war broke out; he failed his medical because of weak lungs, and spent the war years on a cattle ranch. In 1945 he was going up to Cambridge to read Economics, Greek and History.

'My ambition in life was to become a history don at Cambridge. Six weeks before university, when I didn't really know England, I went to church on a Sunday morning and a CMS missionary was preaching. The war was just coming to an end and he made an appeal to young people to go to Africa to try and build things up again. I felt that this was very much something I should be doing. I was a convinced Christian at the time. So I went to CMS completely without parental consent and completely against their will and had a talk with Geoffrey Rogers, the man in charge. He asked me what was I going to do. I said I'd been brought up in the country and worked on a cattle ranch, but history was my main interest. Quite out of the blue—I mean CMS had no agricultural missionaries at all then—hadn't even thought of them—he said, "I think one of the great needs in the post-war world will be for men who are able to help with agricultural work and get people fed." Would I chuck up history he asked, and go and read for a degree in agriculture? I said, a little shaken—I'd flatly refused to do any science at school, I'd absolutely set my mind against it and read classics—that if this really was the right thing I'd be prepared to go and think about it a bit. So I did. I chucked up my place in Clare and applied to London to go to Wye and be an agriculturist instead.

'It came to me from a very strong Christian background and from the very strong influence of a man at school, that one's life wasn't one's own and that one had to be prepared to look to see where it could be used. Up to then I had merely linked this with my particular gifts and abilities. I had been driven to be a swot because I wasn't allowed to play games. Therefore, because I had done reasonably well, and history was a subject I was particularly good at, I would go into history and use my Christian vocation and witness in a university setting.'

He lost his place in the queue for university places in post-war Britain, and went off to farm for a while at the Society of Brothers in the Chilterns. Then he got his place, and met Anne. But he had to start single. CMS regulations in those days were that you did not get married until you'd done a tour, i.e. two years. So he did a tour in Nigeria, just like that—alone. (This astounded us.)

Then, with Anne, he went out to the Sudan. Here he could have lived as others did in a perfectly presentable modern bungalow. But he quickly sensed the yawning gulf between their group and the poorest of the poor they were coming to serve. 'If one was going to be effective as a missionary one had got to get some idea of what people were thinking, and you don't get it by sitting in a mission station, living in the middle of Africa, dressed for dinner.' He and Anne, to the disapproval of their contemporaries 'went native'. He could get no financial support for his ideas at the time, but persuaded his missionary society to let him have two years' allowance in advance; he would live on this and finance his project himself.

The two of them then spent the first two years 'just studying people'. 'We became part of a Kakwa village and lived in a little round mud and wattle hut which we built ourselves for a couple of quid. Anne kept chickens and things like the others and I grew millet and sorghum. We became completely bilingual. We ate with the Kakwa every night and we danced round the fire after dark.' They ate the local delicacies—snakes, locusts, flying ants. They made the first intensive study of the Kakwa and their agriculture, their peak demands for labour, when they were hungry, and when it would be useless to demand labour. 'From this we evolved a pattern of farming which could include cash crops so they could have a chance to buffer themselves against famine which was recurrent in the area.'

At the end of four years they had introduced tea and coffee growing and had plans to resettle the whole of the province of 18,000 people. They had increased the range of food crops and cut down on malnutrition. But they still went on living in the mud hut. They were determined to identify.

In all this, the Carrs insist that they were not trying to be something they were not. They were not trying to be African members of a tribe. They were simply doing what was necessary.

'The Sudan Government had initiated a settlement scheme in the late 'forties and early 'fifties', said Stephen. 'Some of my friends gave the best years of their lives to this and achieved absolutely nothing. Their cotton scheme was completely out of tune with the whole society into which they had tried to impose it. I felt that if we were going to achieve anything in terms of agricultural change we really must know how people think and behave, how they use their time and what their particular desires are. And the only way you do this is by living with them and eating and dancing with them, and crying with them. The other thing was that we were trying to initiate something very new. We were trying to stop the migrant labour to Uganda as their only way of getting money. We wanted to stop the break up of society and families this caused.

'They needed to know and trust you as personal friends and know you as people. Then they were more likely to do what you suggested although it seemed pretty strange. We never had motorized transport. We lived entirely off what we could grow. We never bought food of any kind because we felt that if we were going to demonstrate that there was no need to starve in the southern Sudan then we must not buy food ourselves at all. For seven odd years we only bought salt and pepper which other people did because there was no other salt available. Given a bit of soil and the climate of the southern Sudan you could give yourself a jolly good diet and keep yourself nice and lively.'

Then, just as everything was getting off the ground, and Oxfam, the United Nations and other experts were beginning to offer large sums of money, the whole thing folded. All missionaries were expelled from the Sudan. The Carrs had used their personal savings to get things going. They had struggled for years to win trust, and were now getting money pouring in, plus offers from young graduates who wanted to come and work with them.

The expulsion did not come quickly. At first the Government tried to get evidence to expel the missionaries. 'Everyone had private spies watching them. This isn't being dramatic. The government bribed servants, had people outside windows, this sort of thing. But in our village everyone knew everyone else so there was no possibility of getting a stranger in, and I am glad to say no one in the village thought it was worth the couple of hundred quid the government offered to inform on us. The people of the village made it clear they were not co-operating, and they could not keep any tabs on us. We lived a long way off the road and right away from town. The government officers were not very keen to visit us because the country was still disturbed.'

Eventually a 'reason' for the expulsion of the Carrs was found.

It was claimed that they were in the employment of the British receiving £300 a month for assisting in the training of southern Sudanese guerillas. It was vigorously denied by the Carrs on the one hand and the British ambassador on the other.

So they left Sudan. 'It was eight years of my life just gone,' said Stephen. 'The knowledge we have acquired of the Kakwa is of no use to anybody. That area is now back where it was in the nineteenth century. All the roads and schools are gone.'

The Carrs were finding the hard way what most missionary recruits take for granted today: being chucked out is part of the job. But when the crunch happens, it must be heartbreaking. It says something for the inner backing of people like the Carrs that they straightaway began to pick up the pieces and start all over again. They went down to Kenya, which was in the grip of famine amongst the Masaai, and looked at openings there. Then on to Uganda.

In Uganda, Stephen was asked to look at plans for a farm school for refugees drawn up by the Bishop of Ankole. These had been favourably viewed by a couple of aid officials and quite a lot of money was ready. Carr put in a strong contrary report saying that 'evidence all over Africa proved that if you wished boys to have anything to do with farming under no circumstances let them go to a farm school'. If the Bishop wanted boys to go into farming, the only thing was to demonstrate that farming was worth going into. Carr sent a courtesy copy of his letter to an agricultural officer in the ministry, who promptly roneographed it and sent it the rounds. A copy landed on the Minister's desk. The Minister sent for Carr and said would he like him to back up his words. He could have any site he liked in Ankole.

Carr opted for the poorest, most remote and neglected. 'I felt that I wanted to do two jobs at the same time. I wanted to show that school leavers could accomplish something. But I also felt strongly that given management and direction, even an area that people felt was utterly and completely useless and which they had abandoned could be turned to good account'. All the good land was used, and Carr felt 'It was very silly to have a large county completely empty sttting next to very grossly overcrowded counties.'

In the first month of the new scheme, Carr walked six or seven hundred *miles* around Ankole. There was, as he put it, no

other way of getting around. Mist was blowing over the hills
and cold squally showers soaked him as he trudged across miles
of bracken-covered high moorland. It was empty country. The
climate was too cool, the soil too acid and the mountains too steep
for the common food crops. He analysed soil samples and at the
end of five weeks had a site and a report for Christian Aid. They
confirmed financial support. The Carrs spent a couple of months
in intensive language study, and ironing out the legal land tenure
issues. Then Stephen moved up to the site with his wife and two
young Ugandans and started. They started from scratch, building
themselves temporary beehive grass huts on the top of the hill
for protection.

'There was a feeling,' Stephen said, 'that we would stay up
there in our glorious isolation. It was extremely remote, 55 miles
from the nearest town, 16 miles from the nearest dirt road.
There were no shops. The place was desperately poor.'

But very soon people heard that the Carrs were there, and other
young spirits came up, camped with them, and offered to work
for them. In six weeks they had built themselves permanent
houses out of timber, mud and grass together with the basic farm
buildings. 'We built staff houses for ourselves and our staff and we
put in a bench terrace nursery for just on half a million tea seedlings. We had 150 chaps a day on that. At the same time we had
another 100 chaps putting in 16 miles of road to link us up to the
main road. Amongst all those working, we had 110 school leavers
working as labourers. From those we chose the 29 best ones to
be the first farmers, and they started in January 1964. We still
hadn't got a road in by that time because of the rock blasting.'

They had tremendous difficulty building the last four miles
of road, because it fell away 2,000 feet, and most of the road had
to be blasted through solid rock. They used two and a half tons
of gelignite, but they were still thwarted for several months by
300 feet of solid quartz. 'The nearest we could get a lorry was
twelve miles away. We used to leave at 2 a.m., file down through
the rocks and get to the lorry at 6.30 or 7 a.m. We made the tea
stumps up into 150 bundles and walked the 12 miles back again
all that afternoon. We went to bed just after dark and started
again at 2 a.m. in the morning. In three weeks we moved up
300,000 tea stumps—eight or nine 7-ton lorry loads. It was
terrific for morale. It could have been disastrous for morale if

C

we had packed it in, but having got on top of the situation—and obviously I went down with them—it was great. When the last boys came in and they fetched their stumps from the nursery when they felt like it the first chaps said, "Of course, you people know nothing about it. We, now we were men, we came walking up here, we built ourselves little grass huts, we carried the stumps up 12 miles". I am sure it is the kind of challenge they so much needed. The whole attitude was "You will never get school leavers to do anything. They will hang around looking for clerical work." They responded as you would expect young people any-where to respond. They are proud of what they did and what they achieved.'

In the midst of this hectic activity the Carrs adopted their first son—a coloured child—Christopher. They had never planned to have children, believing that the absence of children left them free to do things other people could not do. 'We submit to physi-cal conditions it would perhaps not be fair to submit children to. But after we had been at Nyakashaka a very short time, a letter came to us from the Archbishop's wife saying this child was going to be born and nobody would take it. She had scoured Uganda for a home. Would we seriously consider whether it would be right for us to take the child? Our immediate reaction was "No". I mean we wanted to remain the way we had been so that we could go into difficult situations and do something. Then we thought "This is nonsense". There is nowhere in Uganda where you can't go and take children and lead a reasonable life. So we talked about this and prayed about it. Eventually we wrote and said, "Right, we would consider taking the child".

'We had been in Nyakashaka a month when we got a telegram saying "Child born. All other people refuse. Please come and collect." We drove down to Kamapla and had a twelve-hour pregnancy, while Anne bought a basket and napkins and a book on how to feed children and things like that. We found ourselves with an eight-day old baby and took him back into the hills again. I think this has been right.'

Carr was a tough taskmaster at Nyakashaka. He made it clear from the outset that only the keenest and hardest workers would be accepted as trainees, and they had to work as general labourers for six months before they would even be considered. In the event, 30 were accepted out of 60 applications. They each got six acres of steep land, covered with trees, and bracken eight or nine feet high. This had to be cleared, all roots removed, and contoured and 'bunded' to stop erosion.

The main cash crop, tea, could yield up to £75 per acre; strawberries, which grew well in the climate, could fetch £1,500 an acre; potatoes were a third good cash yield. The farmers would grow no mealies or other staples: they would buy these with their added earnings from the plains below. But to bring up the protein balance 1,000 pullets were purchased, and a Friesian herd to give milk for the children that were soon to come.

Within a couple of years the hills at Nyakashaka became very populated after being unpopulated for twenty years. 'Other people were moving in. Roads were going up, tea was going in. The whole place was suddenly coming alive. And they knew it was because of their guts and their own hard work, so it certainly had its effect. Then we just went on increasing the numbers of young people each year, and for every group we brought in, others came and settled in around us.'

There are now over 700 farmers in the area. The farmers have their own co-operative to sell their product, and income from the area is heading for £150,000 a year. Individual incomes range from £150 to £310 a year net. And this, it must be remembered, compares with an average farm income in Uganda of £15–£20 a year.

This scheme, in three or four short years, was a success (although Stephen Carr is careful not to use the word: he reckons it has to be ten years old before the full effect can be evaluated). There were a number of reasons for this. There was a sound, even brilliant, technical foundation, and good marketing. There were clearcut rules, which were kept to a minimum. Each farmer signed a legal document before being accepted. And there was security. After three years each farmer received a ninety-nine year lease from the government; furthermore if a farmer was satisfactory for his first six months it was made quite clear that only flagrant mismanagement would lead to expulsion (this happened in only one case out of the 110 trainees).

But far and away the biggest reason for success was the sense of community and purpose. Settlement schemes in Africa have had many momentous failures. In the Government settlement scheme in the Sudan, the settlers were flogged to get them to

weed their cotton. In Nyakashaka the community was created at
first by the common hardship and tough conditions; then by
daily scattered gatherings of farmers at dawn for prayers and a
sharing of news. Because of the geography of the country only a
dozen or two could meet in any one place and this tended to
increase the closeness of group feeling. The settlers built and ran
their own church.

*   *   *

Suddenly, the Carrs left. They were home on leave and announ-
ced that they were not returning. They were pulling up their
roots and moving to Bunyoro, over 100 miles away, with a
totally different climate, language and people, to start all over
again. Nyakashaka was to have another, short-term manager.
Then it was to stand on its own feet entirely.

The settlers were shattered. They just could not understand
why someone who had risen at dawn and worked till dusk for
four years, who had built roads and created a house and gardens
that were as lovely as any in Uganda, should give it all up just
when he might have been expected to enjoy the fruits of his
labour.

But no. The same problems of school-leavers existed with
another bunch of young men. Stephen Carr packed his belong-
ings, and pitched camp with his wife and, by now, two children
(the second child, David, is also of mixed-blood parentage).
This time the land had not been used because it was teeming with
elephant, buffalo and lion. One night in the first week they had
the disconcerting experience of sharing the wall of their tent with
a lion that chose to lie up against it on the outside!

Within a month the next house, built with their bare hands from
elephant grass and timber from the forest, was under way.

It was this delightful new house at Bunyoro that we were
visiting. 'If I had to be sick in Africa I would rather be laid up in
the Carrs' mud house than any place on the continent,' was how a
rhapsodic Canon had put it, back in England. And we could see
what he meant when we arrived for our three-day stay.

'Mud House' is rather a misleading description for the 'Colour
Supplement' Carrs' home. They have simply foregone modern
materials, and built as our forefathers in Worcestershire and

Shropshire did: with wattle and daub. The basic structure is a stout wooden framework over which a fine thatch roof is laid. Then the walls are built up with woven wattle packed with mud. This is coated with a skimming of cow-dung, which leaves a very smooth surface; then the finished walls are white-washed.

The floor, too, is packed mud, skimmed with cow-dung and polished, giving a gleaming shine you could use on a 'Mansion' polish tin. This is covered with split reed matting, giving a warm effect. The windows and doors are mahogany, cut from the forest.

The cost? £140 including labour. It has separate buildings for the living room, bedroom and kitchen.

The reason for these basic materials is more than whim on the Carrs' part. They want to show people what is possible within limited means. Any one of the people they were working with could aspire to a house of the same standard as soon as they were earning. A European-type bungalow, which might have cost about £5,000, was never built; Carr believed it would have created a permanent and insurmountable gulf between him and the settlers.

The Carrs' furniture was of the same pattern. Most of it they made from forest wood; a few precious pieces, books and gifts, had followed them around from the Sudan to Nyakashaka and now Bunyoro. They also grew everything they needed. They bought only salt and oil.

If this sounds puritan, the life-style of the family was far from it. They were happy, self-sufficient, and they lived well. The meals at the Carr household were as gracious and interesting as any we had on our travels. They were not without their sense of humour either. Servants were summoned from the kitchen— 20 yards away—with a miniature hunting horn; a quaint but practical mixture of the upper-class and the bizarre. The deep-drop loo (a covered-over pit, 30 or more feet deep) was resplendent within its own grass hut up the hill. To warn against occupation, and prevent a puffing climb, residents and visitors were invited to fly a flag from a nearby post. Another first for the Carrs.

* * *

What is Carr like as a man? What are his deepest beliefs? Much

of his power stems from his total freedom from and contempt for
money. He just cannot conceive why people should slave for it.
In part this may be due to both his and Anne's upper-class background. Their parents are rich. In part it is due to his early attrac-
tion to the Bruderhof community, which holds all things in
common. 'I had always lived with well-off people and had been
taught that you should give some money away. But the idea that
you should give the jolly lot away, that your standard of living
had absolutely nothing to do with your income, came to me
quite freshly through the Society of Brothers.'

He draws a salary of £400 a year which is paid by Christian
Aid. 'I mean, I say to Christian Aid I would like £400. I could say
I would like £800 a year. If I like, I could say I want £1,200. I'd
get it, it really doesn't make any odds. It seems to me one's
standard of living is governed by what one needs. It has nothing
to do with one's earning power. In the Sudan we had an income
of £96 a year and lived very happily for seven years. Our situation in Uganda is rather different, and there are the children.
So we reckon we need £400 and we get it. I believe very much
that money is a matter of one's Christian faith. As a Christian
one hasn't got a right, merely because one was born white and
born rich and was born with some brains, just to cash in on this
for one's own benefit.'

He takes these views from the need around him. 'I live in a
community in which a shilling is a large sum of money. People
go to great lengths to acquire very very small sums of money for
essential things. A child's education here hinges on whether his
parents can raise 10 Ugandan shillings in six months. And vast
numbers do not send their child to school because they cannot
find this sum.'

Not so long ago he turned down a job at £14,000 a year tax
free. 'The scheme was with the UN—100 families would be
getting 50 quid a year each, £5,000 between them. The manager,
one man, would be getting three times that.'

Carr is not only free of money in his personal life. He is
remarkably free of money worries about his work. This, he says,
gives him an amazing sense of freedom. In the Sudan, 'although
we worked entirely with our own savings, and we often
didn't have twopence from anybody and didn't know where
twopence was going to come from, we were only once under

stress. That was when we desperately needed irrigation equipment to save a large area from dying, and I couldn't raise the money. We spent a few sleepless nights watching the stuff dying.'

Since he has been in Uganda the question of being without enough money has never arisen. 'There has never been anything which I thought right that Christian Aid has turned me down on.' Significantly, though, he cannot find the men. 'I could start three more projects like this tomorrow if I could find the right men,' he told us. 'Money is not the difficulty.'

Carr has an unremitting sense of duty. For him, Christianity very definitely means a surrender of the personal will. 'I wouldn't be here, I wouldn't dream of doing a job like this—I mean I would never have come into this situation if I hadn't been a Christian. I would have gone to a comfortable job in England.'

The same remorseless logic and concept of service will enable them to send their children away to boarding school: 'Either we have to chuck up this place, or our children have to go to boarding school'. It is the same discipline that made him jettison his university career in history. It keeps him in Bunyoro when he knows he is mentally stagnating: 'At twenty-one I had very much greater intellectual ability than now. I have stood outside myself and watched my intellectual ability go down and down for twenty years.' But he stays because it seems necessary; because the grass-roots are where the need is. 'All your managerial ability —it isn't just missionaries it's everybody—is moving out of the grass-roots level, developing plans which may be perfectly sound but which have no hope of fulfilment, because you go flipping round the world and have left nobody at the grass-roots level. . . There's FAO committees. There are United Nations Commissions. Yet, if you look at the export figures, nothing happens at all. Somebody has got to come and do something at this level if anything is to move at all.

'There are first-class research stations with first-class people producing first-class quality stuff which never finds its way to the farmer. You may get your PhD on it and you may make a terrific name for yourself in the agricultural world. But if this doesn't affect anyone's actual farming it doesn't seem to me to make a great deal of difference.'

Carr will follow wherever his intellect tells him he should— no matter what the personal cost. His resolve, his control of deep

emotions, was unnerving. His belief that he was called to serve
for life was central to him and he thought that today's short-term
missionary contracts were one of the basic barriers to real commitment. Even the barriers of present Africanization policies do not
unnerve him. 'We may be chucked out tomorrow. I may say
the wrong thing. But what on earth would you ever achieve if
you thought about it?' Even taking out Ugandan citizenship
may not be right. 'I am not convinced in my own mind that,
much as I would like to settle down and put my roots down here,
this would be the right use of my energies and experience for
the next twenty or thirty years.'

His capacity to pull up his roots has been clearly demonstrated.
When he left the Sudan, 'it broke my heart utterly and completely. I didn't know what to do. But what's the use? If you let
yourself be smashed down by it where do you go from there?
It was very very hard indeed to Leave Nyakashaka. The people
had been warm to us there, they had absolutely taken us in. We
had a particular relationship with many of the farmers because
we had gone there together and we'd slept in grass huts and
roughed it together. We'd had our children there and had an
extremely happy time. I could think of nothing better than
becoming ordained and becoming the pastor, and going on living
there for the rest of my life.'

For Anne, too, the heartbreak is tough. 'Anne puts her whole
heart into getting a place nice from absolutely nothing and in
three years I say "Right, chaps, up" and we leave the lot and she
starts again in the bush. She'll just get this place running com-
fortably—for the first eighteen months she got her water out of
a hole a mile away. Now she turns on the tap and gets good water.
We'll just get nicely settled and I'll say "Right, we move out
again". I'm sure it hurts, but we feel we can't dig ourselves in
and enjoy the place, not in the slightest because we don't want to,
but it isn't right to do so, and to go on breaking one's heart about
leaving things makes you ineffectual. We spend our evenings
planting fruit trees from which we'll never pick any fruit. We
spend out time planning a garden which other people are going
to enjoy. But if you keep on thinking "Well I'm going to leave
this place in three years time" your're not going to put everything into it. You've got to live in a place as though you're going
to live there a lifetime.'

Stephen Carr could never act in this way unless he had a very exceptional wife and a very strong marriage. It doesn't need much insight to realize that Anne Carr is a very remarkable person, in her own right. In the Sudan, before they had children, they shared the work equally. Anne, too, has a degree in agriculture. She looked after the livestock including 12 tsetse-resistant cows brought over from the Congo which she bred up to a herd of 70. She supplied all the children with free milk every day. She ran a big dispensary, and dealt with the medical needs of the community for miles around. She bred poultry, and supplied all the personal foodstuffs for the two of them. 'I would certainly have found it very difficult to have lived like that for seven years by myself.' Stephen admits. 'We would go for six months without outside visitors at times.'

In Bunyoro she looked after the roads and buildings of the administrative compound, ran the dispensary and taught the children. She would 'loathe being an English house wifeafter the freedom of Africa'.

Carr has very decided views on his role as a missionary. 'I don't have two compartments of my life. I don't have a part I call "missionary" which says prayers in the morning and preaches on Sunday and another part of me called "agriculturist". . . . If I cannot give Christian faith to these boys every day, encouraging them to try to grow better tea, then let me pack it in, because then the Christian faith has no meaning. If it only has meaning for the one hour I am standing up in church on Sunday, then it is no use to me. I live my life for 15 hours every day. I don't spend very much of that time saying my prayers and preaching. I say my prayers and preach every Sunday and that is a couple of per cent of my total time. As far as I am concerned the missionary aspect is in the total driving force that makes me do the job at all.'

There has been plenty of teaching on how to be a Christian pastor, or teacher or student, he maintains, but if Christian witness can be offered only through specifically religious activities, 'where is the Good News and what can we offer to those whose days must be spent tilling the soil? I am not training pastors here. I am training men whose Christian life, if they are going to have a Christian life, is going to be worked out in terms of their farming, their family relationships and their community relationships.'

There is a lot of second generation nominal Christianity of the kind we know in England, and Carr attacks, everywhere he sees it, this dichotomy, which has sunk deep into the rural Christianity in Uganda. 'You go to church, you get confirmed, if you are a bit keener you read the Bible every morning . . . and then you go off farming or trading or whatever, which obviously has to do with Christianity.' When his settlers get more prosperous and employ labour 'they immediately come down crunch on chaps and make them work as long hours as possible for as little pay as possible, and then don't pay them at the end of the month— paying them at the end of the second month.' He is able to say to them: 'Look it's quite useless you talking about being a Christian and going to church on Sundays. If you are going to be a Christian the first thing you must do is something about labour.'

So, too, in marriage: 'If a Christian treats his wife worse than a polygamist husband, with no relationship of love, it is of no more value than if he has three wives, and marries outside the Church.'

Also with the care of animals. He is no vegetarian but 'if I have to kill an animal, I kill it as quickly and painlessly as possible. It is an effect of my Christian faith that I believe that the earth, plants, and animals are our responsibility to look after. And this is quite a new concept—to give your cows water when they are thirsty, rather than say they can have water tomorrow—as an outcome of one's Christian faith.'

The Carrs are able to say these things because they live in a community in which everything they themselves do, including their own marriage, comes under close scrutiny. Religion is in fact more part of the lives of the young people the Carrs are working with than in Britain. 'In Uganda, if you are weeding and somebody has been ill three or four chaps get together and go down to weed his garden and help out, and I will go down and a terrific discussion will develop on whether there is revival in East Africa and whether it is necessary to belong to the Revival Movement to be a real Christian. They go on at it hammer and tongs. And it is a perfectly normal conversation they are having as if they were talking about last year's potatoes or the state of the political parties. There is no embarrassment of any kind about discussing one's beliefs. It comes up constantly.'

Young men will sweat from dawn until three o'clock on the

tea project, and then roll out at four o'clock to build themselves
a church. Later they will walk miles to attend an instruction
session by the local catechist. Carr tries to make Christianity
relevant to them. Instead of lecturing them about 'mini-skirts
and drinking too much on a Saturday night', he tries to show that
when the President introduces national service to build bridges
and develop the country, this should call forth a willing Christian
response.

He gets cold comfort from some of his fellow Christians.
Opinions vary between 'How glad I am that you are not just a
missionary, you are doing something useful' to 'I am sorry to see
you are not a proper missionary, I see you get involved with
agriculture'. He sees this as 'utterly artificial'.

One African minister, giving a farewell speech at Nyakashaka,
thanked him for his Christian service. 'The thing he alluded to was
when I slipped down to get him a bottle of communion wine
when he had run out. The fact that I had slogged for fourteen
hours a day for three years to try and give a couple of hundred
lads a new start in life—well this was not in any way related to
Christian service.'

How does he evaluate success and failure? To Carr, the real
significance of all mission work lies in the influence you have on
how others actually live their lives. 'Whoever was responsible for
introducing Kenneth Kaunda to the Christian faith had a profound
effect upon Zambia.'

Carr is determined not to let the incredibly impressive physical
achievements which surround him obscure the point. 'This is not
our main concern. Our task is to help young men who have been
forced into farming to accept it with the enthusiasm which turns
drudgery into pleasure. This involves a profound change in
attitude . . . and it is easier to raise a million young tea trees in a
nursery than produce real change in 20 young farmers.' Increased
income alone will not do this. 'Over-production could make
prices fall, making nonsense of any promises of guaranteed high
incomes. Any permanent change must be based on the richness
of personal relationships and community life rather than solely
on material prosperity. Such as change might bring an upsurge
of enthusiasm which will lead to higher incomes, but the higher
incomes must be the result of a changed attitude rather than the
basis for it.'

One god that Stephen Carr does not worship is the god of efficiency. He knows full well that Nyakashaka would be more efficient today if he were there, but he is quite prepared to let go. He is quite content to see the broadening minds and independence. 'They ask questions. They answer back. They don't just say "Yes Sir, No Sir, three bags full Sir". There was this agricultural officer, a lad of twenty-two. When he came out of agricultural college a few months ago he had never seen a tea plant in his life. He is dealing with 120 chaps, all older than himself, with the same IQ who have been dealing with tea for six years. If he tells them the wrong fertilizer to put on their tea, they would just say "You don't know what you are talking about". Well this isn't what they are meant to say. They are supposed to say "Yes sir, we know you are a very good man, of course your advice must be right because you have been to agricultural college and are a government officer". But they are not simple peasant farmers any more. They are equally likely to have a keen eye for national issues and when they go up to Kampala, to say "Where did he bloody well get that Mercedes? My tax money. I can't get *my* wife to hospital, but *he's* got a Mercedes."'

Had there been any failures? 'Oh yes. Out of the 120 I had to actually sack one because he was such a nice boy. He was such a charming boy, otherwise he would never have got into the scheme at all. Some of the others lasted three months. This particular boy survived a year and a half by saying "Well you know, my mother has been ill, and my father has some trouble". I would never have put up with this from anybody else. I mean it was very naughty of me to go on in collusion with this. After 18 months we sort of looked at each other and he said, "Yes sir, perhaps it is true that farming isn't my work". So I paid for him to go to a commercial school and he writes to me three times a year.

'Then there was this lad who had a wife and three kids and quite a bit of money coming in who had decided the pressure was too much and he would rather go back to 10 quid a year and no pressure than earn 300 quid and have to work. He just said, "I prefer leisure to work".'

But there are very few drop-outs, and Carr attributes this to the rigid selection. 'If we took everyone who came to the door our failure rate would have been very bad indeed.'

Has Stephen Carr ever known real personal failure? We were not sure. If he has, he acknowledges that it would be in the realm of relationships. 'In agricultural terms I have had some successes, this is true. But I wouldn't feel this is carried to all my human relationships. There are plenty of young people at Nyakashaka who as persons find themselves more satisfying to themselves because of having lived near me for three years. But I can look at a lot of young men at Nyakashaka today and say that really I can't see that their experience is richer than it was before I turned up on the scene. Sometimes I look at people and their marriages and the way they bring up their children and the depth of the Christian faith and think "What the dickens did I ever go there for?" '

What does a man like Carr do for relaxation? 'The Christian life should undoubtedly reflect joy. If you are strained to the point where you yourself are useless to others because you just push, push, push, flog, flog, flog this is no reflection of the Christian life. My pleasure is music and fishing, for neither of which I get a great deal of time.' We wondered if this didn't all make pleasure rather utilitarian. It was a sort of aid work. Carr would like more time to fish, it seemed, so that he was more relaxed, and would have more energy for work. 'If I'm going to have more time for chatting to a couple of hundred lads—which is what this place needs—then I feel very strongly that one has got to have some other source of satisfaction. I must confess that my major source of satisfaction comes from farming. For me to see a plant growing gives me just about equal pleasure as listening to a Beethoven symphony. A thing that gives me enormous satisfaction is just to go down there in the evening and sit down and chat—about farming, Christianity, anything . . . just sit down and have a jolly good chat. But I have to come here and write the endless papers on which the world seems to revolve. For the good of my own soul, for the good of Anne's soul, and possibly for the good of somebody else's soul it would be good if one were able to be more relaxed. I can think of no more pleasurable thing than to settle down in a place like this, no longer under the pressure, when one has a couple of hundred people one has to try and get going, and one is trying to get people to do things they have never done before and you must push, push, push. To go into a situation where people are doing things because they now understand them,

are motivated towards doing them, and enjoy doing them—
this to me would be absolutely idyllic.

'I think the thing that has so obviously given stimulus to me in
my work is living in frontier situations. The physical frontier is a
very satisfying one. It gave stimulus to the South Africans, the
Russians, the Americans. One is very fortunate if one is able to
live in that situation of physical frontier in which one goes into
the bush and cuts out a chunk of farm and builds one's own home.
This is something that many people don't have the privilege of
doing. But I think it is sad if your missionary isn't in some
dimension moving along the frontier. This is an essential role of
missions. You shouldn't spend your whole life consolidating
something or some miserable act of someone else. In Uganda,
if you look through the list of missionaries there are 75% serving
in institutions of the past. If you do think that you are merely
keeping something running, I think you have got to seriously
question whether you are fulfilling the role of a missionary.
People see the town as the frontier all the time. But we have not
dealt with the real interpretation of the Christian gospel to the
peasant farmer. This is not considered frontier. The rural areas
have been left in the charge of the indigenous rural clergy—
"good we've finished that job".'

One of the Carrs' strongest beliefs was that the Church was
in grave danger of losing out because of its lack of interest in the
rural areas. 'People will not face up to the fact that in a country
like Uganda 96% of the people live in the countryside,
80% of the population are still illiterate. We behave as though
the whole population lives in Kampala and is sophisticated.
Because the preparation of clergy is in the hands of missionaries
who see the frontier situation in terms of the urban situation we
have got one theological college preparing people for a sophisticated ministry. You have a group of buildings looking like Makerere
University, and a Makerere standard of living for men who are
subsequently expected to come round here and pedal on a bicycle
getting a 100 bob in a good month and 80 bob a month
in others, exercising a ministry amongst a largely illiterate
population. They are taught entirely in English, and it is assumed
that the Holy Spirit only calls to the ministry people who have got
Cambridge School Certificate. They are turning people into men
who will be unwilling to come back to no running water, no

money, no transport and extremely hard conditions of life. When they've had six months of cycling round the bush they say "No thank you very much" and they're into a commercial job at a good salary. This has happened here. We have sent men from here who were committed to village evangelism. They say, "Ah sir, but I would not be spoiled". But they don't come back and settle down, sleeping rough in the huts, and getting eaten by bedbugs, and eating whatever is offered. And it is European Christians who have put forward the plans that brought this kind of training into effect. It is the missionary societies who through their funds and by their supply of personnel make this possible. If you take the statistics, it costs the Gross National Product of 500 people to send one person to Makerere University. I'm not fighting this so much if this produced men who came straight back to the village situation, doctors who were prepared to go and live 70 miles out of town. All right, fair enough. But this is not what happens. People put their entire income into him for years just so that he can abdicate out of the situation altogether. and this being egged on all the time by missionaries who will not face the realities of the economic situation of the country. It is appalling. There are so few people who know. If you said to the average person that the number of employed persons in Uganda percentage-wise had fallen in the last five years, they would say "Rubbish". They'd say "Look at the way Kampala's expanding". But at whose expense? You're absolutely squeezing dry the rural areas. They are poorer than they were twenty years ago.

'What is lacking is Africans with academic education and practical ability. This is not their fault. It is because of the system. If you once get into a secondary school everything is done for you. You leave and go straight into the cloistered life of Makerere. You never do anything with your hands. You never know any practical difficulties. They never get into the sort of situation we get here: building a bridge across a river, or if a tractor breaks down getting their shirts off, which in this sort of situation is something you've just got to do. In England you go and *work* on a farm before you're allowed into university. You spend all your vacations on a farm. You have to dirty yourself and apply yourself to a lot of things. This just doesn't happen here. This is all surmountable. Many Africans have a natural ability and would just pick it up. But the basic thing is that he wouldn't be prepared to pick it up, because his own image of himself is not of somebody who builds bridges across rivers or mends tractors. This does not come into his picture of his role. Therefore you have to import expatriates to do this type of job.'

We felt it was sad in a way that people like the Carrs are likely to be forever peripatetic on the face of this earth. No matter what they do it is unlikely that they will ever have a place they can call home in Africa. Ideally, they would like to stay in Uganda. But under present laws permits are not renewable after five years. 'That, I am assured, means the end of my work in Uganda unless the policy is changed.'

There is a huge problem for the children. What do they regard themselves as? British or Ugandan? 'For me to educate my children in Uganda would be cruel,' Carr says. 'They haven't got a chance, as far as one can see, of making their life in Uganda. Do they start at an extremely inefficient primary school, in the vernacular, for three or four years, meander their way up to secondary school, and if they are any good take school certificate at nineteen? There is every indication that we are going to be kicked out of here. Then they are going to be hopelessly behind to get into an English educational system. We will have said: "Right, because we wanted to keep you with us for three or four years because we liked your company, you shall not have a reasonable education."

'Let me make this clear. I would like to sink some roots down in this place. At the moment, with the government attitude, they would think this super. But I think it would be a dream. Also, I am not convinced in my own mind, that much as I would like to settle and put down my roots, this is in fact the right use of my energies and experience for the next twenty or thirty years. Much as I would dislike it, it might be that I should be free to move out on a wider range and do some other kind of work. I see no point in letting it worry you. We may be chucked out tomorrow. What on earth would you ever achieve if you thought about it? You work on the basis that you are staying the next fifty years. And yet you are realistic enough to know you may go out next year. Obviously if you are concerned about your career and future this is a deadly situation.'

But could the Carrs come back to England? Stephen Carr

finds England hard to take. He contrasts the poverty around him with the grab of England. 'You are met by this barrage of advertising seeking to convince you that that which is totally inessential is in fact vital to your existence. I find this very unacceptable. It goes very much against the grain and I would not wish to be integrated into a society that felt like this.'

Stephen Carr sees his service for life, and in that he is different from most modern missionaries. He believes that the attitude 'for life' makes a big difference. 'A missionary can move into situations where effectiveness can be out of all proportion to the sort of power behind you. They are in a position where they are free to develop themselves, come to the top and then have a profound influence on society. But this isn't done by someone on a four-year contract. Immediately you are up against language. Without language you cannot be effective. It's getting extremely difficult now to get young people to come out for life. And this "life" business comes into it. There's little thought of "I'm prepared to commit myself through thick and thin". For me this is for life. Whether it's comfortable or whether it isn't. Whether I'm thanked or whether I'm not. Whether it's dangerous or whether it's not. If you are really going to be effective it doesn't necessarily mean staying in one physical place. But I think it does mean staying within at least one cultural pattern. The trouble is if you mention a missionary society to most Christians they fly a mile.'

Stephen Carr once wrote down his criteria of a good missionary. These included:

'Commitment: offering service irrespective of pay, housing, security, comfort, gratitude, promotion, status. A willingness to move or change jobs at the expense of any of these factors, and to be prepared to offer a long term of service rather than a period which coincides with your own convenience. To base service on the needs of others and not your own satisfaction.

'Involvement: entering into the life of people rather than offering impersonal advice or service. This means learning a language (or several languages) and social customs. It means adapting yourself to other people's eating habits and food. It means ordering your home so that people feel entirely at ease in it. It means using your leisure among the people you live with rather than your own compatriot group.'

D

What does one make of such a man? Weeks afterwards we found ourselves asking the same question over and over again. There is not the slightest doubt in our minds that his project is one of the most successful in Africa. The entire budget for Nyakashaka was only £32,500, and £25,000 of that was returned by the settlers to start his next project at Bunyoro. He has an exceptional degree of planning and efficiency. Against all expectations he has successfully convinced young men who expected to be doctors, lawyers or teachers to rejoin the land, and to date only two out of 110 have left the first scheme at Nyakashaka. He has got a keen Christian community going, without the presence of priests or ministers.

And the 'absolutely unsquashable, disgustingly self-confident' bit? Well yes, one can see what the person meant. He sets a pace that few others could follow—or would want to. He knows where he's going and goes there with a relentlessness that is a bit like a machine. He is hardly a man you would choose to relax with or fail under.

But then we've all got our vices. And, well, what can you say about Stephen Carr? He just is—in the very nicest way—unsquashable.

NOTE:
At the time of going to press, Stephen Carr had been seconded by the CMS to work for the World Bank in the Sudan for a year. He is in charge of their agricultural work in the war-ravaged south.

CHAPTER FOUR

Skyscrapers, Slums and Piety

A stranger to modern Africa will lose his image of the dark continent pretty quickly. The skyscrapers, the sweeping architecture, the modern hospitals, the endless city traffic will soon convince him that the pace of present development is going to push tribal Africa further and further into the background in the next few generations.

The cities are large, and getting larger. Nairobi 'city of flowers', must be among the most beautiful cities on earth. It has grown immeasurably since Independence. The swamp that ran through the city has been drained and turned into exquisite gardens. African businesses are expanding. There are TV programmes, computers—and many more whites than ever before. A small town like Meru in northern Kenya has built ten self-help harambee secondary schools in the last few years, at a cost of £100,000 in African donations.

The élite guiding these developments represent a new Africa. They face problems of management, industrialization, and political freedom. Above all they face the embarrassing gap between their own position and that of their tribal countrymen. The poverty gap is wide and yawning wider, with all the dangers of a revolution of rising expectations.

Cities like Nairobi and Kampala may have their beautiful new boulevards. But they also have an ominous bulge of shanties on the outskirts as thousands of school-leavers crowd in looking for jobs.

It is a problem that is likely to get worse before it gets better. At present only 29% of youngsters go to school in Uganda, and already the system can't cope. Governments make urgent calls for Africans to go back to the land, but their pleading will be to little avail as long as a man can get more as an office sweeper than he can toiling in the sun on his 6 acres.

Mercedes are thick on the ground. Expensive housing contrasts starkly with the lot of the poor. Grumbling, resentment, conflict are never far away. Those who care would like to see cuts in ministerial salaries like those made in Tanzania.

Local African Christians who speak out are few, and under pressure. The Reverend Henry Okullu, at one time editor of the Christian newspaper *Target* in Nairobi, is a good example. His predecessor, an expatriate, was forced out of the editorship because of a series of controversial articles on oathing. Okullu was appointed in the belief that a national would behave himself.

'I made it quite clear I would only take over to continue the policies of the paper and its previous editor', Okullu says, 'but they kept hoping.' He quickly made it obvious he would be no yes-man. He fearlessly campaigned against renewed oathing in the highest circles of Kikuyu, and attacked the Nairobi city council for callousness in its treatment of slum dwellers. His Board were asked to dismiss him, but they refused.

The churches as they exist today are in the main conservative, pietistic. Leading African churchmen like Professor Mbiti, head of the Religious Studies Department at Makerere University, can see enormous dangers in this: 'I am afraid the Church is going to suffer very severely for this conservatism.' He believes that the new generation are just not going to submit to the kind of haranguing they are often subjected to in the local African churches. There is a dogmatism, an authoritarianism that people like Okullu just won't accept: 'This belief that we have the truth, the key to heaven, this absolutism is our trouble. In a way it is true. I believe it absolutely. But do I impose it on people?'

Most of the missionaries we talked to saw this. But too late. By now the indigenous clergy are in charge. And they like the pomp and circumstance, pay and privilege that go with power. They also display all the conservatism of established churches in Britain. Trevor Huddleston told us that he was far more radical than his clergy in matters such as the use of drums in church. They had been brought up to believe this was evil, and tribal and wanted to keep the Western style music.

In some ways, the missionaries have really failed the emergent churches. A growing number of separatist churches have hived off from the major denominations altogether. There are now over 5,000 different independent churches amongst 290 different tribes in 33 African nations, and membership runs to 6,900,000.

One hundred bodies with 300,000 adherents are forming every year.[1] Their reasons for separatism are many; some started because they couldn't stomach giving up polygamy; some are hardly recognizable as within the Christian tradition. All, to a degree, are a rejection of white dominance and a desire for linguistic and cultural control of their own. This is strikingly shown in South Africa, where the separatist churches, with a membership of over 4,000,000, far outnumber the official membership of the Protestant and Catholic churches combined.

The churches have, in effect, been caught napping by the complexities of modern Africa, as they were caught out in the industrial revolution.

'It is so sad', one missionary wrote, 'that at present the Church is a poor but respectable relation of the élite, with clergy and laity alike aspiring only to become more respected members of the élite; while if a real revolution of values does take place (as it has in Cuba and Tanzania) the Gospel will again be marked by the fact that the Church will be associated with the reactionary and the conservative.'

He is asking for exacting standards. There *are* such men among the Church leaders but they are few on the ground.

Significantly, it was men like these who most wanted to see an influx of the right kind of missionary. 'We need them to open minds, to fend off a stifling conservatism.' They were the ones that saw most clearly that it was not so much a case of putting the Church right as getting the Church to help lay Christians as they shoulder the crucial tasks facing them at their secular jobs.

The middle road, the road of honest doubt and fair, brave criticism is the hardest road to follow. 'Every time I think over these things,' Okullu told us, 'I feel the dilemma of the middle position. I don't know the answers. But true Christianity for me is to live in a state of creative tension. And once you become outspoken you must face what comes.'

★   ★   ★

Our first introduction to the kind of missionary working with these problems was the Reverend John Mockford.

---

[1] *Concise Dictionary of the Christian World Mission*, Lutterworth Press, p. 9.

We arrived at his house one Sunday morning, tired after several days of interviewing. He was late, or we were early, and we sat on the driveway cursing our luck at spending a blazing hot Sunday waiting to interview a parson. When he arrived, zipped up in a dog collar and broiling in the heat of it, he greeted us heartily without enthusiasm.

We went inside, to be faced with a huge 'Jesus loves you' placard. Our first impressions were not favourable. Hours later it emerged that he, too had thought: 'What a way to spend a Sunday being interviewed by a couple of globetrotting journalists.' But by then he had removed the dog collar and changed to a gay blue African Katenga shirt, and he had told us 'You can relax now. You're not visitors any more.' One of the joys of this sort of assignment is that sometimes you really *meet* people; you communicate.

John's mission was to the élite in the cities. 'Most of the problems are at the top. I feel this very strongly,' he told us. 'It's an extremely difficult task which in many ways would be done better by a senior African. One or two outstanding men could do it, but they're engaged in other activities.'

He sees a large part of his job as straight race relations. 'I am one of the only Europeans who belong to the African Uganda Club. Most of the Europeans congregate at the higher priced Kampala Club. I go to the Uganda Club and talk to people and have a drink. I also visit their homes—it's a privilege, the reverse of England. The Englishman sort of bristles and says 'My home is my castle'. The African counts it a great honour if you visit him.

'Most of the élite are carrying burdens beyond their expectations and it's stretching them to the utmost. Our task is not to ask them to do church work, but to support and strengthen them in their secular careers. There is an awful lot of feathering of nests going on all over Africa, and we want to build up a Christian nucleus of men of integrity who will understand the needs of the whole community because the great danger at the moment is that the gap between the rich and poor is widening. These are people between two worlds. There is a Kiganda proverb that "he who serves at the feast without getting food will proclaim later that it is a bad feast". Everybody expects to get something out of the feast, but as long as they are in fact serving at the feast nobody is going to say anything. Everybody regards a certain amount of feathering of nests as legitimate. It's the same with wages. It is traditional even to people who I thought were really Westernized that a labourer doesn't work for wages. He works for subsistence. If he's hungry enough he'll work for 80 shillings a month, the thinking goes. So why on earth does the government pay him 150 shillings?

'The leading men really have grown up in mud and wattle huts. They've still got all that behind them whatever they've learned as well. It's a big thing for them to sort out and this is where a lot of Christian thinking has got to come.

'The Church is still so rurally centred. Even your top Christian laymen tend to be more orientated to putting the Church right than helping the Church find its role as a servant of society. And yet we could have a *terrific* effect on society. Christians number the great majority in this country. Uganda is far more Christian than England.'

The poignancy for men like Mockford is that 'In the West we're pulling down churches, and people in the West will only give to social problems. Here we are *under* churched. We have only got three modern churches in the whole of Kampala,' But the difficulty of the situation for John is that he recognizes all too clearly that this job can only really be tackled by Africans. 'Europeans are the wrong colour. We would like to be involved in social problems like hostels and housing but we just have not got the manpower.'

Is Stephen Carr the wrong colour? we asked. 'No, but Stephen Carr is the kind of slave-driver that will not last terribly long in Africa. His time is limited. The amount Europeans can drive is very limited. There is a sense in which Africans will ask you to, and want you to, but if you do it they'll *hate* you for it. And whatever you do will bear the stigma of that hate for years to come. And this is just as true in the Church as outside.

'We ought to de-escalate. We ought to get fewer and fewer. This is not liked at home, not by the home mission staff, not by the Church here of which a number of leaders are very much paternalistically orientated.

'Ultimately we've got to realize that Uganda is going to be an African country that nevertheless wants to live in the Western world. It's got to be helped somehow to hold on to that double vision. This is going to be frightfully difficult. We can do bits and we can help in bits, but ultimately it has got to be Ugandans who work it out for themselves. Otherwise it won't be genuinely theirs. So ultimately we've got to get out. I suspect it's a big mistake that we hang on thinking that we've got the only thing that matters, efficiency. I think they have to find out about efficiency but they possibly have to get rid of us to see how important it is.'

Angela, John's wife, gave us an amusing example of the kind of racial group attitudes they have to overcome. 'You see, we look at Africans with a kind of block concept. We say "Oh! An African". Well in the same way our stupid ways of greeting people, our stupid ways of insisting on weird time relations, our ways of having breakfast one way round and dinner the reverse. You know, with breakfast we start with something that looks like pudding and end with something that looks like meat. All of these are lumped together as the odd "Kisungu" (white) way of doing things. All our perpetual rush and our bad temper. It's all Kisungu. And until we go they won't be able to disentangle it and see what's Kisungu and what's actually part of business efficiency. We don't give enough to personal relationships. We are far too blunt.'

In working with the élite, the Mockfords enjoy being immersed in a wholly African environment. 'When we came out here four years ago we were met at the station by three Europeans and no Africans. When we returned we were met by Africans. Now we feel that if we're in trouble we go to Africans first. We are isolated from the crowd at Namirembe, and we are the only Europeans in an African set-up. We came to a project initiated by Africans.'

Angela enjoys the crossing of the cultures. 'I go to the market, discuss the potatoes, bargain about the onions and generally have a natter. I get much better value if I do, and it's fun. But I have to be in a certain mood to tackle it. It's a bit more lengthy than just seeing your cut and taking it out of the supermarket, but I think it's worth it.'

People like the Mockfords almost have to unlearn their own history. 'In the old days a missionary had to understand the culture in order to become more one with the people,' John commented. 'Nowadays it is almost the reverse. We have to help the Africans

in the city to become a part of the city and to be Christians in a
secular society. Do you see the irony?'

We felt the Mockfords had an almost impossibly tortous path.
'You can be accepted as you, yourself,' John said, 'while you as a
part of a group are rejected. The key to acceptance is not trying
to get other people to accept you but to accept other people first.
You look with new eyes at your own culture and drive for efficiency. Our failures are when we rush things, when we don't
respect the African enough. I think I have learnt the terrific value
of people as such. I've learned that the weakest most distintegrated
person must be accommodated within a team. I've learned that
the only thing you can do in a situation is just hold on. I think
the African, once he has worked through this period, is going to
have a tremendous amount to give to the Western world: a
re-baptized sense of community. Not his old community which
was very strong, but there is something new he is coming to.
I have a hope that something will emerge, because there's more
life, more sharing together in the down-town shanty areas, and
our senior African Christians will say: "All right, we've got to
go through these transitions. But let's ease the changes. Let's see
people as people even if they have to lose their job."

'This may come to be as sick a society as the West. But at the
moment there is hope. And this is the thing that's missing in the
West. There is *terrific* hope. This is not the place for the despon-
dent or the disillusioned.'

Working in the urban situation, working with the élite and
living so close to poverty, the problem of the right standard of
living is one that exercises the Mockfords. 'We find it an embarrassment—both ways. We are the poor paupers to the white
managing directors up on the hill. And we are the rich uncles of
the Africans in the shanties. This is just one of the things we have
to live with. We find it hard to part with possessions. This is
something which is "Kisungu". It's in us, like everyone else.
I don't think we find it easy to accept the relative poverty of
being missionaries. But when you see what the African pastors
are living on . . . Again, when you compare the other people who
were with you at Cambridge and what they've got, you do get a
twinge now and again. But if I was challenged to live in a shanty
area I couldn't take it. Although my Christian and socialist
background would say "yes", I couldn't take my family into such

conditions. And anyway, even if the European gives up all his possessions and lives among the shanties, he can always pull out again. People say we need a prophetic ministry here and we do. But the cost of being a prophet is a very high one and there are very few prophets about.

'In the last resort you are yourself. You can't rid yourself of that Cambridge accent. You get to the freedom of being yourself. But you've got to make the effort of identification.' We both said we would find it very hard not to be accepted like this, but the Mockfords seemed to take it on the chin. 'I don't think it's difficult to understand really,' Angela said. 'I lived for a short while in post-war Germany and I am half German so I could hear what people really felt. They were longing to get rid of the occupying powers. Well think of the amount of time we've been occupying here, and the way in which Europeans have impressed on the country that they are superior. I don't think it's at all unreasonable that they are so very anxious to see our backs.'

We stayed with the Mockfords long into that Sunday. For lunch, tea, supper. The picture that emerged of a quite ordinary person, changing and shaping up to the complexities of the racial melting pot, showed that the job of the white missionary in urban black Africa is anything but simple.

*   *   *

That week we also went to see David Williams, who was facing some of the same problems. He too, was working near Kampala, as number two to an African in religious broadcasting.

David lived in a large modern bungalow surrounded by lawns and flowers. His home was comfortable, with modern furniture and fittings, and a modern kitchen. His wife, Wendy, told us that people at missionary meetings back home just could not accept that David and she had a higher standard of living than they did in Bromley. 'Go on, Wendy, we all know what you suffer and go through,' one woman told her. But what they go through is no longer connected to disease or physical discomfort. It is for them the agonies of communication. To them this is the central problem of the modern missionary.

'It's a question of personal relationships,' David told us. 'It's a newly independent country yet in so many ways there's lack of independence. The expatriate must see how he and the African can relate. And it's terribly difficult to know that. Sometimes you sense the whole time this feeling of irritation: "When will this man get off our back?" I don't think you resent it. This is part of the challenge to the missionary. Years ago the missionary came in and said "I'll live on that hill over there. It's got a nice view". When you go to these places you'll notice they've all got beautiful views, they could go wherever they wanted, that's what it comes to. They put up their house. They got their people around them. They taught them and the world revolved around them. The privations they had were very real. But the tensions today are almost impossible to talk about. If I had to choose when I'd be out I'd say—now. I'd much rather be out now because it seems such a worthwhile thing that we're trying to go through.'

A lot of missionaries were aware that they had a terrible image, and David was very anxious that we didn't misrepresent him as a missionary. 'Just supposing you were to do a potted thing on me as a missionary,' he warned, 'it would tend to work against the main aim of my work, which is not "missionary work" but an aspect of the Church of Uganda's ministry." '

Why then, did he first come out as a missionary? 'To some extent it was the old romantic idea that I wanted to help spread the Gospel and show Christ overseas. But whatever one feels at the beginning, when you get out here this is the sort of reality which you quickly face.' Wouldn't this be a dampener to most new missionaries if they looked at it like this? 'I think if it's put in the right way, there's something infinitely more worth while to come out and bat in with the local church. In any case in independent Africa it's almost unthinkable to say "We have come because we wanted to come". You see we haven't got a right to say that any more. The Church has its own Province with it's own African Archbishop. Our only pretext for being here is that we've been invited.'

One of David's most difficult roles is being number two. 'There have often been times when I itch to go into the radio studio and do a few experimental things. But I haven't. I've left it completely alone except to be available when the African director wants to consult me. I have felt "All right, there isn't as much creativity as I want, but it's got to come from him". It's got to grow naturally because if it's just the expatriate exploding all his ideas you paralyse the Ugandan. He says, "Yes I under-stand". But he doesn't understand at all and you haven't been fair to expect him to understand because you come with a whole series of assumptions from what you know in the UK. It's very difficult to remember that the assumptions you're bringing come from there and you haven't discovered them here. This business of discovering how we relate, it's everybody's problem. There is a kind of fear that in some way we are still manipulating them.

'Again, there are things in traditional African life which we didn't bring here and which we've tended to stifle. The early missionaries looked at many things and said, "My God, the devil incarnate!" Today we're saying, "Hey wait a minute, that isn't so evil after all. It expresses something that maybe needs to be re-expressed." But we don't just throw it away.

'I think the 'seventies are going to be a very testing time in Africa. We are exploiting the African even when we're not doing it intentionally. If you go to a meeting with a group of expatriates you come out of the meeting and you think "We never really stopped, we never really slowed down. We just talked in a foreign language. They never had a chance to get a word in!" We have got to get beyond the point where the European is a threat, where the African thinks that when you say something threaten-ing you are being sincere and when you say something concilia-tory you are being devious.'

Didn't all this make the missionary an ordinary sort of bloke, fitting in with any intelligent social programme? 'One of the greatest tasks a missionary has is to try to show people at home that he *is* a very ordinary and normal sort of Christian, and that even some of the motives that have brought him out have been such things as wanderlust and a feeling that he'd like to go abroad and go to Uganda. Some of the reasons that bring a missionary to Uganda are exactly the same as other expatriate workers—just a feeling that he'd like to go somewhere else. If there is a special problem it is trying to be a Christian in a culture which is not his; and it is increasingly less his culture because independent Africa is desperately trying to rid itself of unnecessary culture from the East and the West. The expatriate appears as someone who is clogging up the works in discovering this culture.

'Mostly you have to have some specialist knowledge to do a job that is specifically needed. But more and more over the last year or two I've come to believe that the real significance is the person, being who you are and trying to make what kind of contribution you as a person can make. It isn't just a case of me, as someone with a heritage of several hundred years of Christianity, wanting to come and implant this in some paternalistic way.'

*   *   *

After meeting John Mockford and David Williams and their families, we began to realize that 'missionary' was a loaded and not very useful word. If we were to do a useful job in saying what 'missionaries' were, we had simply got to get rid of our preconceptions and look at these people just as people, look at their aspirations, what job of service they were trying to do, and what attitudes they brought to their work. Then and only then might we begin to get a glimmer of what 'missionary' means in a nineteen-seventies context.

From the Mockfords and the Williams, with their intellectual worries, their almost neurotic concern about race relations, we went on to look at life in the shanties, and work that other missionaries were doing amongst the most poor and down-and-out. The Mockfords and the Williams, we felt, were not wrong to be so preoccupied about race and human relationships. One only wishes that, somehow, they would be left alone, like John Mockford said, to be themselves, accepted for what they are, Cambridge accent and all.

*   *   *

The next missionary we saw was involved in the urban situation, immersed at the stark point of human need. One sensed that at this level worrying about race and relationships took second place.

He was at work at a community centre, St. John's, set in the midst of Pumwani, a slum district of Nairobi. 'Read Dickens, Africanize it, and you have Pumwani,' we had been told. Pumwani is perhaps the most depressive slum in Nairobi, situated a bare two-and-a-half miles from the city centre, the affluence, the flowers, and the tourists. In one of Africa's most beautiful cities, it is a great embarrassment to the City Council.

Pumwani is the other side of the coin of industrialization. People crowd in from the rural areas, into the poorest, cheapest houses attracted by the lure of the city, of jobs, hoping against hope to escape from the grinding poverty of the country-side; they find themselves trapped instead by the poverty of the town. Pumwani was first developed to house workers who were stranded when construction of the railway stopped at Nairobi in the 1920s. At first standards were reasonable. Each family was given 1,500 square feet of land, with a maximum allowance per building of 15 people. Today the large mud buildings crowd alley-way to alley-way. The average packs in 27 people. One house holds over 100, and there are many examples of two or more families sharing a 15-foot by 10-foot room. There are 11,000 people and a density of 250 to the acre (with single-storey buildings). There are 15 latrines and 8 water taps: one to every 1,000 people.

These are the statistics. We found the living reality to be deeply shocking. Our first inclination was to run, to escape. The place felt sultry, violent in the heat. It was no surprise to find that 75% of Nairobi's serious crime took place there. On a hot day the narrow alleys between the houses were dusty, with a trickle of effluent down the alley gutter. In rain they were awash; with mud everywhere. Going into the gloom of a doorway, you had to take care to pick your way past a hot jiko and avoid the rain from a leaking roof. There were ragged children, jobless men, on every corner. Pumwani was for the old, the poor and those who just hadn't made it.

But there was colour in Pumwani, as so often with poverty. There was a strange lure; bright kangas drying on the lines, woodsmoke, laughter, a sense of community. In the evening the area took on the air of one enormous gay night club, with the local girls practising their principal trade as 'self-employed business-women'—as they put it.

Poverty like this brought all sorts of problems. Pumwani had few married people. Those Africans who lived there and had white-collar jobs tended to send their wives and families to the rural areas rather than bring them up in these conditions. The young, almost inevitably, were unemployed, for there were no jobs. Some 200,000 children leave primary school in Kenya every year, and only 10% go on to any kind of further education. Most of the children leave at twelve or thirteen, and are not allowed to work until they are sixteen. In Pumwani they have no income, often no parents. They roam the streets, hanging around the hotels and markets, scavenging and drifting into petty thieving and prostitution. They learn nothing that could be useful to an employer, they forget whatever learning and discipline school gave them.

The situation for the old is hardly better. The ties of the extended family, which are so strong in rural Africa, break down to a large extent in the urban township. Many of the old folk in Pumwani are reduced to sleeping in passages or on verandas.

One wondered how any helper could make meaningful inroads into such a problem. The Municipality of Nairobi had its own plans, which were to bulldoze Pumwani to the ground and start afresh. 'The best solution to the problem is to leave Pumwani as it is and forget all about it, but we as a Council cannot do that,' said Town Clerk J. P. Mbogua. These plans aroused a lot of opposition and hostility because most of the inhabitants of Pumwani could not pay the new rents of 230 shillings a month for two rooms in the new flats. (Rooms in 'old' Pumwani cost 20 or 30 shillings each.) Rehousing may well break something of the community spirit, too. 'Shovelling the poor away in the name of hygiene,' as one local editor put it, could mean that even worse shanty towns will appear.

In this situation the Church did seem to be making a dent on the problems through St. John's Community Centre. The work started in 1956, at the end of Mau Mau when the Christian Council of Kenya launched five community centres in the worst areas of Nairobi. CMS missionary Charles Tett was asked to head up the St. John's Centre. He was a no-nonsense kind of leader who felt that far too much of the Church's time in England was 'spent worshipping the death-watch beetle.' He came out to a Kenya still very much under colonial rule. (Visiting an up-country settler area with an African bishop in the purple he was told, 'You can come in, sir, but leave your boy behind'.)

Tett's first step was to organize a teenager's club to attract boys off the streets and give them broader education. But he soon realized he was only playing with the issue. In 1958 he decided to launch a scheme of technical training. He gathered support from various government authorities and the Church and with a capital of £100, mainly spent on tools, he started a carpentry workshop in a disused schoolroom. Then, with gathering support and £2,500, he employed six African teachers and opened several classrooms. Each year after that a new workshop or classroom was built by the boys themselves. By 1965 the reputation of the Centre brought 480 applications for the 80 places. Today, there are workshops for carpentry, painting and signwriting, sheet-metal work, welding, mechanical fittings and electronics, plus classes in English, maths, science, civics and religious knowledge. There are 144 boys, 72 in each year, and there are plans to take the Centre up to an enrolment of 216, increasing the course to three years, including the Kenya Junior Secondary Examination. And there are now 2,000 applications for the 72 places each year.

The intriguing thing to us were the low costs. In the nine months before we were there the training centre had cost only £12,200 and of this £6,000 had been contributed from the sale of the boy's own work, and a further £2,000 from fees.

This expansion would be striking enough if the churches had taken the cream of educated young people. But they had done the opposite. The Centre in Pumwani was situated in the middle of the worst area. The most important qualification for entry was a hopeless background. The 2,000 would-be entrants came to the Centre because 'for many of them it was their last chance' according to the Director, Tony Idle. 'Most of them come because they can't afford the fees elsewhere. In town they pay 700 shillings a year, almost twice what we charge, and there they get no practical experience.'

Many of the boys had incredibly difficult backgrounds. Some lost their parents in Mau Mau. Some already had a criminal record. One boy, for example, was picked up by the police for persistent thieving. His mother was a prostitute and he had been thrown out of home as an embarrassment to her trade. He had lived by stealing all his life. He had even stolen to find the money for his education. The Centre suffered. Tools were stolen, even a major burglary planned. 'But what do you do?' asked Tett, 'do you write him off as a malingerer? It's no use preaching. You just talk. Somehow you have got to get through.' In this case he did get through, and the boy found and held a good job as a maintenance mechanic. He had saved his money and bought his mother a piece of land so that she could establish herself as a farmer.

Something of the spirit of the place comes across in even a brief visit. Our first sight of the boys, fit, athletic, dressed in khaki drill with CITC badges on their shirts, showed an obvious esprit de corps. The contrast with the hopelessness just across the street was marked. The place seemed to have captured something of the prestige of academic education, which is rare in Kenya where the greatest difficulty is to persuade young people that farm or technical work is at all worthy. Nor did they simply practise theoretical exercises. The boys worked on actual car repairs, made tubular chairs for local churches and schools, and carried out contract welding. They could take home some of their own carpentry to their parents. They could see they were making something useful. Above all they knew that when they had finished their course most of them would step straight into jobs. By 1970 the Centre had helped 800 boys to find employment.

The training at the Centre is tough, but it probably has to be. 'If a chap arrives two minutes late in Nairobi, he'll lose his job,' said Tony Idle. 'There are crowds outside every factory gate every morning looking for work. Everywhere you see "Hakuna Kazi"—No Work.'

In 1966 a similar centre was established by Tett in Mombasa, with an intake of 144 and a grant of £200,000 from the West German churches. In 1968 a third centre was opened as a pilot project in Kisumu, the main port on Lake Victoria. This time the centre trained girls as secretaries, after a survey had shown 3,000 young girls unemployed in the midst of a perpetual shortage of trained office staff. Ten girls were trained to start with, and now, with a grant of £15,000 from Christian Aid, the centre has expanded to 24 day girls and 24 boarders.

In the last resort the value of these places probably depends as much on their indefinable spirit as on any training. The wife of the Vice-President of Kenya, opening the Kisumu Centre, stressed this: 'Skills alone are not sufficient; in the long run it is the character that counts. The foundations of this nation will not be laid upon the skills of its citizens, but rather upon the character of its people.'

This came through in the attitude of the staff we met. Tett was convinced that the effectiveness of his Christianity was the measure of his caring and identification: 'This, I find, is easier to

E

write about than it is to practice. It affects the whole pattern of daily life and is revealed more in our attitudes of mind and heart, than in any techniques we can devise or any programmes we can organize.'

This kind of missionary work is new, and comes in for criticism from older-school evangelists. When it was first started it was labelled 'sub-Christian'. Even now people ask 'Why don't you get on with first-line evangelism?' Tony Idle answers this by saying: 'God is more interested in how a chap does his job on Monday than a few mumbled words on Sunday. Integrating work and belief is central to us. You don't preach the Gospel on an unemployment card. This work gives the lie to the charge that missionaries are interested only in saving "souls". We are interested in the whole person.'

CHAPTER FIVE

The Fanatics

Our story so far sounds like an apologia for missionaries. What follows should dispel any such illusions.

We were having supper in the missionary guest house in Kampala, soon after we first set out on the assignment. A lean, crew cut, short-back-and-sides American fundamentalist from Zaire called Chuck Davis was holding forth on the dangers of liberalism. Modern Christian thinkers like Teilhard de Chardin, Tillich and Bonhoeffer he dismissed as 'sub Christian'. The World Council of Churches was a 'pernicious body' which was undermining true Christianity. He wouldn't accept free medicines from them in case his work in Congo was morally compromised. 'We see the medicines as a bribe. We say "These ecumenical people are bad fellows— they're bad boys—they're trying to trick you." And so we stand firm.'

You name it, he seemed to disapprove of it. Hellfire, damnation, he believed the lot. I can still see him clutching the edge of the table, knuckles white, leaning forward with a jutting chin. Lips thin with tension he argued with the young girl sitting opposite. She was an innocent volunteer. 'But don't you think God is just as much interested in helping when we see need?' she asked sweetly. It was a red rag. Ten minutes later she would ask again: 'But don't you think . . .'

The main theme of his onslaught was that most modern missionaries had got the wrong end of the stick. They were nothing more than social workers. Evangelism was the task.

Across the table a second member of the company was developing blood pressure. Helen was going quietly red. There was that look she gets—the lull before the storm. A short end to the trip threatened. But with mighty restraint she kept her cool until supper was over.

Then she exploded. 'It just makes a mockery of any notion that missionaries have learnt anything,' she said, when we got back to our room. 'How can we write with understanding facing a granite wall like that?'

Later that evening, overcoming natural sensibility, she asked Davis if he would talk to a tape recorder and give us an interview. Although it was the night before a long and gruelling landrover drive back to Zaire, he agreed, and stayed up well past midnight expounding his philosophy.

As Davis related his story, we had to admit his personal courage. It transpired that he had arrived in Congo with his wife and children in 1964 only a few days before the Simba rebels captured his mission station in the 1964 rebellion. The Simbas had rounded up 298 missionary and civilian hostages, and were debating whether or not to shoot them when the Belgian Red Dragon paratroopers closed in. In the confusion that followed the Simbas opened fire on the crowd of men, women and children. He and his family saw people riddled with bullets in front of them. Trying to escape from the carnage, a fellow evangelical, Paul Carlson, was machine-gunned as Davis helped him climb over a wall. When it was all over they left for Switzerland and never thought they would see Congo again. But, incredibly, they believed God was calling them back. 'I could have been disobedient—there's a great mission field in America with this college uprising, and that's where I'd like to be.' They came back and approached the border with a 'real tight knot in our stomach, real nervous tension'. We bet.

But courage can be closely allied to fanaticism. And we could find little sympathy for the views he was in Africa to propound. Davis was a missionary of a fundamentalist body operating mainly but not exclusively in Zaire. Its *Statement of Faith and Affiliations* portrays quite clearly the line they are pushing. Amongst other things, it proudly claims to have dealt 'the death blow' to a United Church in East Africa. It believes in the 'divine, verbal inspiration and infallibility of the Scriptures' and their 'absolute and final authority in all matters of faith and conduct'. It believes in the 'eternal blessedness of the saved and the eternal punishment of the lost', and that men are saved 'through faith, not by works'. It is proud that it has warned Church leaders 'of the danger from false teachers who deny the word of God and who seek to substitute a false ecumenicity for the true unity of the Body of Christ'. Likewise, it does not 'approve association with the Roman Catholic Church on any organizational level having to do with Church matters', and 'rejects union with the World Council of Churches'. The Statement spoke of 'a doctrinal position of historic fundamentalism, conservative and evangelical'.

Chuck Davis, as we soon realized, had not been expounding individual idiosyncracies at the supper table, even if, as another writer put it, 'When he gets around to the subject of wickedness his denunciations were no less than thunderous . . . and when he spoke of sin and Satan, his voice simmered with rage.'[1] He was straight down the middle wicket on a brand of religion that makes most outsiders shudder.

It is integral to this kind of authoritarianism that there are absolutes. As Davis put it: 'I say it is more fun to go to bed with a different woman every night. Why the morality unless there are absolutes? Unless there is a God who says "I'll judge you because it's wrong—I'll judge you physically. I'll judge you psychologically. I'll judge you emotionally. And besides that I must judge you eternally because what you are doing is hurting other people who are created in my image." ' A lot follows from such attitudes. Children, for example, were to be disciplined: 'The rod may kill him but it may spare his soul from Hell.' The role of women was strictly per St. Paul. 'If my wife is so busy that she cannot be a mother or encouragement to me when I need her and I'm dead tired, well she's not really fulfilling her scriptural role in marriage is she?'

Roll on Women's Lib!

*　　*　　*

The next time we ran into this kind of conservatism was in a little tract published in Nigeria and Tanzania entitled *20 Awkward Questions and 20 Frank Answers*.

This booklet says that 'No one can deny that the happiest, most stable, and most enduring marriages are those in which both husband and wife come to marriage with no previous sexual

[1] III *Days in Stanleyville* by David Reed, Collins.

experience with each other or with anybody else.' I would think about fifteen or twenty million people in the United Kingdom could be found to deny that one for a start. Again, 'Living together beforehand does not help at all in showing whether the two will suit each other in the life-long partnership of marriage.'

Not at all?

Again, in like vein: 'Many a young man who has "sowed his wild oats" has reaped a terrible harvest of bitter memories, disease, and knowledge that he can never have the best things in life. And many a barren woman faces loneliness, shame and barrenness because she "had her bit of fun" when she was young.'

How many?

We found it incredible in 1968, when this was published, that a responsible Christian body should put forward the argument that couples should refrain from premartial sex because 'there is no absolutely certain way of preventing conception' and that 'many babies who become blind soon after birth and a large number of children who die in infancy or who survive with some defect are the victims of disease brought about by wrong doing.'

Even when you get married, sex, apparently, remains a fairly grim pastime, for even then 'we must not indulge to excess' (Why?) and it is apparently 'so wonderful and sacred that we ought never to treat it lightly or jokingly'.

Is the sacred and the wonderful never light or joking?

The document is honest enough to admit that all this is 'easier to advise than carry out'.

*　　*　　*

We did not, in fact, meet a great deal of this kind of thinking in East and Southern Africa. Perhaps this was due to the fact that, in the main, we were meeting medics, teachers and agricultural-ists, rather than clergy. The clergy are still conservative, but the great majority of them are now Africans, and because they grew up in an era when the Church was much more authoritarian they have emerged more dogmatic than most of the present-day missionaries. The changes that have been sweeping the training colleges and theologians in Europe have hardly affected the local African clergy at all. Several times on a Sunday we passed local churches where the African pastor was holding forth in a voice that was recognizable as a harangue, whatever the language. Places like Kampala are already experiencing a drift from the churches as educated Africans refuse to sit and listen to such sermons.

The other reason that we did not come across many people of the Chuck Davis stamp was that in the main we were looking for the modern missionary who was aware of issues of development, and able to communicate in a fairly meaningful way with people back home. It was inevitable that such people would suggest that we visit their friends.

But whilst we met no one else of quite such forceful persuasions, we came across many examples of a muted authoritarianism. There was, for instance, the case of the two nurses at a hospital we visited who were sacked because there was a *suspicion* of immorality. Two men had been found, fully clothed, in the nurses rooms. That was enough.

Brother William, whom we describe in another chapter, admitted that large numbers of the local faithful were excommunicated, because of non-adherence to the Church's rules. And in many other places we felt that the strictness was still there, even if subdued.

When we got back to the United Kingdom we were curious to know just how representative the brand of fundamentalism we had met in Chuck Davis really was, and we came to the conclusion that, in the aggressive form in which we had encountered it, it was not common amongst British evangelicals. They are too polite. Even fundamentalist British missionaries are embarrassed by it. The nearest equivalent here are reputed to be the Welsh Baptists, but even they seem milder and more reasoned. This particular brand of out-and-out fundamentalism is, it seems, identified with the Americans, in particular the Americans from the Baptist 'Bible Belt' in the deep south. These are the boys who have invaded Zaire, Nepal and Latin America in large numbers.

The only person who was blunt with me was the General Secretary of one missionary society who said, 'But I wouldn't expect you to understand the Christian faith. It is a faith revealed to those who seek it. Are we, then, to believe that a person can wake up one day and say that the Christian faith was now reasonable and that he had become a Christian?' He was more pugnacious than the rest. For the most part, as soon as we indicated that there might be things about Christianity which were of dubious benefit, people shut up like clams. They seem less responsive to criticism overseas. And in this sense, missionary work is bolstered in primitive regions through lack of criticism.

To put it bluntly, there is no one to laugh them out of court. The more gullible the reception, the more they are encouraged.

One of the most dangerous things about religion, at least in its extreme forms, is the conviction of certainty. One quite pleasant missionary described commitment to me in these terms: 'Once you are committed to Christ, he has the last decision and guides all you do.' The trouble is, who makes that last decision? And who interprets it? Divinely guided individuals have done some very different and some very funny things with their guidance.

*　　*　　*

The most extreme example we read about was of a missionary called Stan Dale, of the Regions Beyond Missionary Union. Dale is a recent martyr, who was murdered by hostile tribesmen in New Guinea in 1968. During his time amongst the hill tribes, he and his followers were strongly resisted by the local people. He described how, when they first penetrated the area they were met with groups of shouting men: 'I could not understand what they were shouting about but their gestures were eloquent enough. "Don't come here," they were saying. "Get out! Go back, go back."' But, continues Dale, 'it was too late to go back; eighteen years too late by that time. I had not come all that way in time and distance to turn back at the word of men.' Unwanted, he persevered and after two years was beginning to attract a number of people. 'But we had not yet realized the power of Satan and sin, the grip that fetishes and superstition held over the lives of the people.' People at the meetings sidled confidentially up to him and said 'We have been coming for a good while now and listening to your words. When are you going to pay us for listening?' As soon as he had a handful of converts he encouraged them to get their villages to burn all fetishes. 'We gathered round the pile of fetishes, sang some hymns and thanked God for giving the Christians courage to destroy them.' Neighbouring villagers were angry. They were not amused at what they probably saw as a direct threat to their security, and promptly murdered two native Christians. Dale called in the police, and set off to recover the bodies. When the police withdrew, Dale went on. 'I knew it could be extremely dangerous. . . At first I walked slowly, carefully investigating the track in front of me before proceeding, for every bush could conceal an enemy and every thicket an ambush. Then the Lord gave me an assurance of His protection and I stepped out more briskly.' That night the protection must have become a bit shaky, for he was attacked and struck by five arrows which pierced his thighs, arms, bowel and diaphragm. Undaunted, he 'laughed aloud derisively and called our assailants to run away home'. A policeman who had followed him obligingly fired some shots, shot one of the assailants, and the rest fled. Then followed an incredible gruelling trek back in which the wounded man twice gasped 'Leave me alone, I'm dying.' But then, 'The Lord's own word came to me, "I shall not die, but live and declare the works of the Lord" and I clung to the promise as a staff.' He recovered, thanks to a Missionary Aviation plane and some brilliant surgery, and went back to carry on the work. Two years later tribesmen finished him off, putting almost a hundred arrows into his body.

Martyrdom? Or rough justice attendant on insensitivity to local opinion?

It's a matter of opinion.

But one thing is fairly certain, and that is that only someone totally convinced of the superiority of their beliefs and culture could have behaved as Dale behaved. To the fanatics, life is a battleground between Right and Wrong, in which they have personal communication with the headquarters of Right.

Let me give another example, this time from a letter to prayer supporters of work amongst the Falashas Jewish sect in Ethiopia: 'It seems to me that we are going out at the command of Christ to re-open the campaign against the Falashas, and that you are not only going to supply us with most of our ammunition, but are also going to take part in the fighting. . . The Falashas seem so ripe for plucking. Materially speaking everything is working towards their conversion. BUT WE HAVE YET TO SEE REAL SPIRIT GIVEN CONVICTION OF SIN.' (Their emphasis.) You may say that this is a vehement but harmless expression of enthusiasm; fight the good fight and all that. But then in the same literature you

find a passage that demonstrates a hardness towards 'wrongdoers':
'There was one rather sad incident when one of our student
teachers, the son of an evangelist, took examination papers from
another teacher's room and showed them to his sister. When this
was discovered he and the girl both denied it and lied more and
more about it. I gave him the opportunity to come clean but he
did not take it and eventually had to be dropped from his job.
He is now trying to get into the Gondar High School and his
older, rather unstable brother is trying to get a job. Do pray for
this family because apart from anything else his parents are going
to find it difficult supporting the family without his help and supporting him if he gets into the Gondar school. They are reaping
the fruits of the lack of discipline in the home.' In other words,
you sack a guy, then ask people to pray for his family who will
suffer. And justify the whole thing by the throw away about
'lack of discipline'. Didn't Jesus forgive sins?

The problem is a deep one. Christianity is basically an exclusive,
authoritarian religion. 'No one comes to the Father, but by me'
(John 14: 6 RSV). And no amount of contemporary liberal
wriggling can remove this hard core fact. It is no surprise to find,
as we found in one Baptist Missionary Society prayer letter,
the locals (in this case in Zaire), totally confused by the imposition
of a culture several thousand miles and two thousand years
removed. Here were some of their questions. 'If Jacob could have
four wives, why cannot we have more than one?' 'As Jesus
turned the water into wine at the wedding in Cana, why did the
early missionaries teach us that it was wrong to drink wine?'
'If we are all descendent of Noah or Adam, why is there such a
difference between the white and black races?'

To outsiders, there are many things that don't marry.

It may be maintained by some that attitudes we have described
are not really harmful. A bit 'off', may be: not quite the thing,
but as long as no one takes it too seriously, rather good for the
morale of the troops.

We would suggest that on the contrary, it is wholly pernicious.
Harm is done even to those who refuse the blandishments. Their
belief in their own culture is taken away without any solid re-
placement. Those who accept the message in full, proceed to alter
their lives accordingly. Their language, their thought forms, their
rhetoric become moulded on a way of life wholly different from

their culture, rooted not even in the contemporary Western or African world, but in the thought forms of a couple of thousand years ago. They are more likely to know about Bethlehem than the slums of Nairobi; they are more likely to be concerned with battles against their hitherto natural sexual urges than about the necessity to establish morality in contemporary local business.

Sam Keen, in his brilliant little book *To a Dancing God*,[1] describes the disillusionment that he felt on finally setting aside his Bible Belt upbringing. The following extracts from 'Memories and Expectations of a Pseudo-Israelite' express this:

> Before I was six I had walked through Judea, Galilee, Capernaum, Bethlehem, Jerusalem, sharing a dusty road with Jesus and the disciples, finding at the day's end the comfort of a footbath, bread and olives in a humble home. And what a rich time it was to which I belonged! . . . From papier-mâché models I learned the architecture of the Holy Land, and from bathrobe dramas its way of dress (and at recess there was milk and Graham crackers). I learned of Deborah's heroism (but not of Molly Pitcher's) and of the judges and kings the Lord raised to lead and chastise his people (but not of the judges of Blount County who helped to keep whisky illegal and bootlegging profitable). . . For the time being, Jesus required only gentleness and abstinence from the obvious sins (smoking, lying, stealing, swearing, going to the movies, questioning orthodox theology, sex, and a frivolous enjoyment of the world). With all seriousness and commitment I prepared myself for the hard task of living as a heavenly exile in the midst of a sinful world. A wayfaring stranger travelling through this world of woe must be armed against the seductions of this age. There is always the danger that cheerfulness might break in and dispel the serious truth that all men are sinners whose only hope is casting themselves on the mercy of Jesus Christ. . .
>
> The crisis came in the early hours of a February morning within view of the Harvard Yard. The armies of the Lord faced the army of Truth. On the one side was all that I had believed about heaven and earth and my dazzling aspirations toward purity, sanctity, and obedience to a known God. On the other side a restlessness in the loins, a handful of facts that would not be denied, and a wilderness which hinted of both terror and adventure. The issue was so drawn for me, that the choice was between remaining a Christian or becoming honest. The armies defending the Holy

[1] Fontana, 1970.

Land fought to the last before yielding. Exhausted, I slept. I awoke at noon in Cambridge, Mass., USA, and after coffee and rolls, began to create the world.[1]

This mirrors Richard's experience so completely that we are sure it must speak to many other people. For years you are brought up with a conviction of certainty, in a thought-system that is military in its division of the world into good and bad. Then one day you question the whole edifice, and when it tumbles you face a total void. Across the gap of years you have to re-create a rationale afresh. You realize that human existence ceases to be a problem to be solved and becomes a mystery to be explored. You realize that this is your life; meaningful existence is in the now, not in a mythical past or future.

Richard may be able to pick up the pieces, seeing others around of similar intellect and education living meaningful human lives. But what happens to the simple African convert who wanders to the big city, or comes to England and grows up? He is much more vulnerable and has even more cultural changes to adapt to. Time and again Africans have told us of the crashing disillusionment they have experienced between the picture painted in their formative years, and the reality of the world as they find it as adults.

One of the dangerous things about missionary fanatics is that they can still command wide audiences in some underdeveloped countries; audiences that have not the knowledge or intellect to answer back. I am reminded of a story told me by Mildred Neville of the Catholic Institute for International Relations. She was visiting one of the more conservative and authoritarian bishops in West Africa. He showed her a vast audience of young Africans chanting the Te Deum in Latin, then proudly confided to her that actually they were mostly Moslems and didn't understand a word anyway. But the Church had got them within its grasp. Mildred thought this was monstrous. So do we.

[1] *To a Dancing God*, Fontana, pp. 8-13.

CHAPTER SIX

Non-News

There is a story—allegorical or not we don't know—about the two sub-editors who were tired of writing sensational headlines for every piece of copy that came before them. 'Let's for once write it as it is', one of them said, 'Let's see which of us can write the non-headline of the night.' Next morning a small news item appeared, entitled 'Small earthquake in Chile. Not many dead.'

Most missionaries are like small earthquakes. They don't make news either. And one of the dangers in writing a book like this is the natural temptation to concentrate on the magnetic few. It is a mistake that has been made before: there are over fifty books on Dr. Livingstone.

Simon Barrington-Ward, Principal of Crowther Hall, the Anglican missionary training college in Birmingham, voiced his fears about this whilst this book was in draft. 'Who did you naturally go for when you came up to our place?' he asked. 'The colourful, the youthful, the gay; those who would "catch on" with the public, whom one could, so to speak, sell. But are these in reality,' he asked, 'the people whom I can see as likely to be doing the most crucial or the *most* valuable job? It may well be the quiet, unphotogenic person in the corner, the worthy couple who seemed just a bit on the pious side, who have every bit as important a role, if not a more important role, to play by virtue of their very self-effacingness.'

The people who most impressed him, he said, as having the commitment and the humility and indeed the sheer self-discipline and guts to stick out what may often be a very demanding unromantic coping with difficult personalities, with a precarious situation, with misunderstanding and criticism were not necessarily the ones who would make the most obvious dramatic story. 'The missionary's role is, if I may be paradoxical,' he said, 'first and foremost to be secondary. They are very seldom the colourful pioneers in the old sense, even the Stephen Carr sense. They are essentially background figures, indirect influences, who like good community developers stimulate others to action and leadership. It isn't necessarily the larger than life or even the young, fresh and eager types who really make the running.

'Look round,' he went on, 'at some of the faces at missionary conferences. Some people have been refined and deepened by glimpses of terrible deprivation, frustration with Church institutions, taxing climates. The men sorted out from the boys, so to speak, aren't necessarily what I might be tempted to think of as Exley heroes and heroines.'

Fair comment. And we will take the Principal up on the point and try to describe some of the people we met whose quality most impressed us—not their deeds, but their simple piety, their steadfastness. We met 87 missionaries on the first leg of our trip in East Africa. Here are five groups and individuals who with no disrespect, are 'non-news'.

*   *   *

Gordon Marshall was our host for a sizeable part of our East Africa trip. He is a pilot with the Missionary Aviation Fellowship, a group of flying missionaries who have set themselves up to perform the often mundane service of ferrying missionaries to and from their bases in the remoter places. He had not asked for the job of ferrying two agnostics around: it was just part of the job.

He impressed us, quite simply, by his kindness, which we found the more significant given his background: that of a former pilot in the South African Defence Force. He ferried us more than 2,000 miles in a week: and during stopovers, snatched meals at airstrips and guest-house breakfasts, he told us something about himself. He had grown up in South Africa, where his views as a child were the same as most of his white compatriots. 'I would never have called myself a racist, even if I did have the usual South African feelings that we were, I suppose, inherently better.'

As a boy, he was a Christian and admired missionaries: but he had no desire actually to become one. He became instead the youngest officer in the Air Force, and in 1950 he volunteered to go to Korea. Then one day he got separated from the others. 'I was perfectly safe and heading south along a railway line. Then I saw refugees walking down the line. There was snow everywhere. I was flying low and as far as you could see both ways there was this line of refugees, four or five deep. They had no shoes and so few possessions. I had this overwhelming experience, and said to myself: why am I using this aeroplane when there are people like this? And I questioned: How can I use myself as an individual?

'I didn't become a missionary then' (he went on to complete 100 military missions), 'but after I had been back in South Africa a few months I got a letter from Steve Stephens, a missionary pilot in the Sudan. His eyesight was failing and he asked me—just like that—if I could come and take over.' Gordon went, but not without misgivings. 'Actually I had no intention of leaving the Air Force but when I got this letter I just had to do something.'

His life today is very different. He flies missionaries to remote areas, brings their children back for schooling, ferries bishops to conferences and keeps the wheels of missionary work going in three countries. But his heart is in the pioneer work his service does in remote areas on the northern frontiers of Kenya. Once every three weeks he leaves for Lokori to back up the work of a Dr. Anderson in reaching the most scattered parts of the Turkana tribe. 'We take out provisions for a whole week, medical supplies camp beds, the doctor, a nurse, an evangelist. At Kalabata, the first place where we land, there are no houses and we circle for five miles around to tell people we are coming. We camp under the wings of the plane. When the people arrive the doctor starts them singing Turkana songs to Christian words. In this way he'll talk to them and after half an hour start a clinic. That will go on for three or four hours. The next day we move on, and so on for a week.'

MAF run similar services on Lake Victoria, and in Somalia, in each case starting the service first and finding the money and support later. Gordon puts all new MAF pilots (there are 50 planes around the world, and he is responsible for training in Africa) through 80 hours of test flying and 200 checks.

We found it hard to conceive of Gordon's background as a man of war. The contrast couldn't have been more striking. He was so utterly kind. Living, travelling beside him we saw the simple, absolute faith of a person who was in many ways a quite ordinary Christian. He read avidly every book that could possibly help him in his faith. He read his Bible daily, copied out copious notes of sermons. Each day before we set out he conducted prayers in the cockpit (asking us each time if we minded). He was absolutely painstaking and conscientious about the safety and comfort of his passengers.

But it was the little things we so valued. The spontaneous, outgoing warm way he greeted everyone we met (and everyone seemed to know him); his ready offers of baby-sitting to help our work; his going out of his way to help us out between journeys after arriving back from many hours' flying.

Most of all we liked his prejudices. It was only after we had been with him for days at a time that he confessed to us that he had resented the whole trip. He blushingly admitted that he couldn't see why he was wasting MAF space on a couple of agnostics. This had troubled him deeply, then his very resentment had troubled him, and finally he prayed and read his Bible until he worked through it and came to the conclusion that God in his mysterious ways was probably using us whether we liked it or not.

We left Gordon with a sense of sorrow at parting.

*   *   *

Father Richard is next on our list. We met him when Gordon Marshall flew us down to Masasi in remote southern Tanzania. Far from being a charismatic dynamo, Father Richard is in the nicest possible kind of way, an old-fashioned drop out. 'Last year,' he told us, 'I went outside the bounds of the parish for the first time in four years.' Father Richard (or 'Daddy Richard' as our children insisted on calling him) could not by the remotest stretch of the imagination be called 'with-it'.

He is parish priest of Mkomaindo in the remotest part of southern Tanzania. This is part of the Anglican Diocese of Masasi where Trevor Huddleston was bishop for eight years. It is a poor parish, with its roots in hundreds of mud huts spread over many square miles. Father Richard has sunk himself totally in the life and the life-style of the people he serves. 'We came out to live like Africans,' he says. And when successive policy makers, like

Huddleston declared that expatriate clergy should not be needed he simply decided to become a Tanzanian. 'I don't ever want to go back to England. I am very happy.' He is a bachelor and lives in a small tin-roofed home that is half-way between a hut and a house. Some things have just gracefully faded into the past. His books all have that vintage dusty look of bygone college days. His furniture is hand-made. Even the bed is plaited grass on a wooden frame. There are piles of old magazines for the children to read. His clothing is two surplices, a pair of trousers and a couple of pairs of socks. A Tanzanian friend sent him a shirt: but he hasn't got pants to match so he never uses it.

One morning, before dawn, we dressed and crawled into a Land Rover to go to see Father Richard 'in action'. We travelled eight miles, walked half a mile along a track in the forest dotted with huge snails and 'tube-train' centipedes and came to a large, tin-roofed church in a clearing. The light was streaming through the trees on to the dew and we sat down to wait. Over the next hour (or was it two?) Africans in their bright cloths trickled into the church, and settled on their knees at prayer in a scene that seemed as timeless as the trees.

Then down the path came Father Richard on a bicycle, surplice blowing in the wind. He, too, had set out at dawn. All the kids ran out to meet him when he arrived, and he talked: to us, to the catechist, to everyone—with a face that was creased in a weathered smile. When the time seemed right (and he went by no watch) he went to the church and started Mass. And there cannot be a much lovelier, more heart-tugging place to hear Mass than in such a setting.

After Mass he would return to his simple mud hut by the church. It had a bed (no mattress) and a chair. There he would stay with the people for the next three days or so; helping in the communal clearing of the land around the church, taking services, talking, being.

How do you evaluate such a man? Should you try? Here was someone who had taken on another culture. He was veritably a 'father to his people'. And colour made not the slightest scrap of difference. 'I have to look for English words now.' Educated young Africans, who inevitably left the villages to further their careers, found him the one link with their past. They could not write to parents who could not read, and Father Richard's small

F

desk was piled high with long letters from young people all over
the country.

Masasi is a backwater into which people like Trevor Huddleston come as whirlwinds. ('He never stood still for five minutes,'
grinned Father Richard.) Is it in the quiet eddies of a parish like
Mkomaindo that the Church is finally measured?

*   *   *

Devout and believing Catholics always seem to us to have a
brand of saintliness all of their own; the last three people on our
list of non-news makers are all Catholics, and they all possessed
this, the genuine softness and mystery that seems to come for
some people when they take the three vows of obedience, poverty
and chastity.

Forgoing freedom, the creativeness to use money and possessions, and the beauty of sexual relationships can either turn a
person into a bitter, dried up shell; or it can, in a strange way,
liberate them. If your choice of action is partially circumscribed
by loyalty and deliberate corporate choice, if you are freed from
the encumbrance of possessions, and if you choose to love many
people without the ties of family, this can bring the greatest
freedom of all. A Jesuit friend of ours says that of course the vows
are hard: but having taken them, the three apparent denials are
precisely the three areas in which he has greatest freedom.

*   *   *

We were nearing the end of our East Africa trip. We were at this
stage beginning to feel that we had had a surfeit of all things
missionary. It wasn't that missionary work wasn't good. That
was the problem. It was so good, so earnest, it made you want
suddenly to shout out loudly in the guest house corridors. The
whole business of 'self control' somehow became a bit cloying.

So it was in a fairly rebellious mood that we set off, on a very
hot day, for the Roman Catholic Maternity Centre at Thika,
40 miles from Niarobi.

Perhaps something of our feeling communicated itself to the
three Sisters who met us, for they were charm itself, with more
than an ordinary sense of humour.

'Are we wrong to feel the way we do?' we asked Sister Christopher, the oldest of the three, after we had talked a while. 'Are a lot of missionaries rather joyless, perhaps especially the evangelicals? Are we right that Catholics in some sense seem better at going out and meeting life?

'I think it's fair comment,' Sister Christopher replied with a grin. Then, more seriously, 'Everyone remarks on the serenity of the Orders. This comes from an absolute certainty God is behind us. We've never taken the joy out of our religion. We believe we are all made in the image and likeness of God; anti-social behaviour, deviant ways—we're still part of the family and his children. We're all so weak anyway, we can't judge.' And then the grin again: 'Go to any jail, you'll find it full of Catholics. Perhaps the worst scoundrels and rascals belong to the Catholic Church. We never hide them.

'We're not afraid to laugh at ourselves,' she went on. 'Nor,' she said, and perhaps this is significant, 'at our Church or confession.'

Sister Christopher is a quiet but busy little person. She is the sort of steady committee type who, because of a predilection for what most people avoid, finds herself landed with every volunteer task going. She teaches religion in six secondary schools, visits the Thika prison on Sunday, organizes shorthand, music and English classes on week-nights, a women's craft industry in the mornings, two youth clubs at week-ends. She serves on the local Red Cross, Child Welfare, YMCA, and Women's Association.

As she showed us round the wards, accompanied by Sister Monica, the Matron, the infectious gaiety of the place came across. It was one of the most cheerful hospitals we had seen. Maternity hospitals are often happy places, but there the sheer colour and friendliness was especially obvious. All the beds had different coloured bedspreads; there were flowers all round, in the gardens, in the hall. The nurses' standards, too, were impressive. There was a noticeable briskness about the place in coping with a dozen or more deliveries a day. Yet despite the efficiency, there seemed little of the sense of officialdom that you seem to get in many British hospitals.

The three Sisters were members of the Holy Rosary Congregation, which has similar works in South Africa, Zambia, Sierra Leon and the Cameroons. They were of widely differing ages.

Sister Christopher joined the Congregation in 1933, from a wealthy family. In those days, she said, you obeyed the Mother Superior implicitly; authority came naturally. Now the younger Sisters questioned everything. She welcomed this, but was quite satisfied that Sisters in earlier times fulfilled themselves: 'We had a much less complicated outlook.' She had seen service in 'Biafra' in the Nigerian civil war, and in South Africa. She could not get back to Nigeria after the fall of Port Harcourt, so came to Kenya.

Sister Anne, in contrast to old-time Sister Christopher, joined the Congregation in America, attracted by missionary work in Africa. She is young and beautiful, and has friends who are hippies. She has a lot of empathy for the present younger generation. 'The hippies I know are searching for peace and for what is real. It's a round-about quest for God.' She thinks this era will produce good missionaries: 'Young people are not inhibited. Those entering our Order now are generous.'

Young or old, all three of them welcomed the changes ushered in by the Second Vatican Council. 'It's marvellous,' Sister Christopher said. 'We're getting a good rocking of the boat. It won't do us a bit of harm. What is time in God's eyes? Up to the present the Catholic Church has been on the defensive. But now the whole world is rocked by change. Yes, we're going to lose a lot of priests—but not so many when you see the total numbers. Celibacy is not the issue. It's authority. Paternalism is ending.' She welcomed the sense of freedom of her new simple habit in place of the starch and ankle length of the past. 'You've no idea what a performance it was.' But she wouldn't like to do away with it altogether. 'It's a sign, a part of your witness. I think the wearing of a habit gives people confidence.'

Some of our early prejudices against authoritarian Catholicism were perhaps due for revision. Intolerance is giving birth to tolerance. Sister Christopher, for example, now works in complete co-operation with the local Salvation Army: at opposite ends of the theological spectrum. She works with unmarried mothers (often the bulk of pregnancies) and with prostitutes without any trace of judgement. Irish Sister Monica, the Matron, even tells the story of the Saturday night dances where 'sex was rising' and there was pressure to stop the dances. 'Sure an' they like to feel each other a bit,' said Sister Christopher, with worldly acceptance.

A lot of people feel that nuns give up their whole lives, but that's not the way Sister Monica looks at it: 'I wanted to do something worth while. I thought, I'm making a sacrifice, why not make a bigger sacrifice and go to Africa? No. That sounds rather negative, doesn't it? That sacrifice part. I suppose the only real sacrifice was that I loved my country. But now I'd never go back by choice. There's more need here. Anyway I'm happier in the life and that's what most people are looking for, isn't it? People think we are tied down, but really we are free, you know.'

The Sisters were agreed that preaching gained little. Sister Anne said that if her life didn't portray Christianity, nothing else would be much use. 'I hope to live as Christ showed us how to live, rather than by preaching.'

It is a high standard to be judged by. A standard that does not rely solely on the traditional institutions of the Church.

You soon realize, when you are on an intensive trip of the kind that we were on that it is really only the people that make the going. After you have wandered over this maize demonstration plot or that, after you have looked around your twentieth hospital ward and tenth X-ray lab, you rapidly feel you have seen the lot, plus or minus a bag of fertilizer or a technician or two.

It is the people that makes the difference. Somehow goodness, laughter, serenity don't weigh in the wall charts. In the ordinary missionaries we have described, these qualities were there in abundance.

But they will never make news.

CHAPTER SEVEN

Land of Apartheid

We spent the next few months in South Africa, where we stayed on a farm in the Eastern Transvaal belonging to Helen's mother. We had the time to be introspective, to write, and to organize forays into the surrounding African territories to visit many more missionary and aid projects.

Helen grew up in South Africa. This is where she had learned to disrespect the Church for all it did not stand for. This was the land where many of the most ardently religious groups were white, Calvinist and repressive. Strict Sunday-best, little girls in white hats and white socks, these are still the order. And it is these groups that practise the most cruel strains of apartheid.

At the time we left East Africa we were beginning to find the atmosphere of constant goodness more than a bit cloying. The 'have a drink' bonhomie of Johannesburg was at first a welcome change. No Calvinism here, just a bustling materialism. Our immediate reactions on arriving were a welter of confusion; shock at the godless, godless affluence, relief at the escape from goodness. Richard sat down at the time and 'blew his mind' on the subject. A lot of what he then wrote would be modified on sober and cautious reflection. But these reflections were true for us then, and for this reason are worth recording in their impetuosity.

> There was so much about missionaries that I responded to yet so much that repelled me. By and large we met few saints. More realistically we met a group of people who were most noticeable for their trying. They desperately wanted to do the right thing. They earnestly strove. They did nothing by halves.
>
> I reacted against this earnestness. When I met the real saints— like Father Richard in Masasi or Sister Christopher at Thika— this reaction faded away, perhaps because their religion includes

a sense of being at peace, a reconciling, loving force. Very little attracts me that is bustle and earnestness. I admire the achievements of aid, but in one sense the crusading Canons of the Church, the fire-eating social reformers leave me totally unmoved. They seem to me just dressing up the stridency of radicals in religious garb.

It is strange that on the whole trip, not one person really communicated their faith to us. In some people you could see that there was something there that you wanted, a quality of living, a sense of peace. But no one could talk about it. They could talk about social problems. They could sprout clichés from the Bible. They could deliver sermons, but they could not reach out to me as a person; could not communicate the thing which presumably was the most precious to them.

If they had, perhaps we would have been converted.

What I rebel against most is the two-box concept of life. Good and bad. All this comes back again and again to judging. I know there will be protestations of innocence, but no smoke without fire. It isn't without accident that most people we have spoken to about missionaries have singled out this one quality, this devastating vice, as the hallmark of the missionary. The missionary head-quarters, the training centres, have done their damnedest to drive this vice away. John Taylor and others like him have said accept, accept, accept. But if the Church wants to make headway, if it wants to get through, it has got to go through the profoundest revolution. It has really got to throw its superiority out of the window.

Time—and meeting many more missionaries—has mellowed this reaction but not removed the grounds for the criticism.

* * *

We wanted to have a look at the missionary situation in South Africa. For many years South Africa has had a fairly large number of overseas clerics and others working as guests of the Anglican, Catholic and other churches. Many of these—from the time of 'the turbulent priest' Trevor Huddleston—have been involved in clashes with the Government. In 1964–6, when Richard was manager of a South African relief organization, we had travelled extensively to mission stations and hospitals in Zululand and the Transkei in South Africa. We had photographed dozens of victims of malnutrition in the hospitals, had met many of the staffs, and caught something of the atmosphere that pervades mission hospitals even under the apartheid regime. Yet their work was not really recognized even within the churches.

We had realized then that many of these men worked under impossible circumstances. I remember one Anglican clergyman in Molteno, in the northern Cape, telling me over lunch that I was like a visitor from another planet. He had not had a visitor in years who talked as though justice and equality should be the norm. He had already been branded 'communist' for doubling his servants' monthly wages from 30s. to £3. 'What do I do?' he asked me, 'I could empty my church for ever with one sermon if I said what you are saying.' You have to compromise to carry on.

People like Dr. Anthony Barker at Nqutu in Zululand have struggled on for years, meeting the very real needs of the people around them and knowing all the time that to some extent everything they do props up the system they detest, and can even be used as a show piece for that system. But such missionaries believe that they cannot leave a man to die because to help him is to play somebody else's fiddle.

Mission hospitals such as Jane Furze in the Northern Transvaal have gone through agonies knowing what to do. If they help newspapers, such as the liberal *Rand Daily Mail*, to report the prevalence of malnutrition in their area, they are pressurized and could have their work stopped. The multi-racial hospital staff at Jane Furze used to play tennis together until some informer pressed for action and the threat of removal of government grants stopped this. Barker, at Nqutu is perhaps tougher. His staff sit down for meals together, and visiting government officials, if they do not like it, have to eat elsewhere.

On this occasion we started to make plans to continue our tour in South Africa, to visit afresh all these old friends. But we chanced to meet one, a hospital doctor, at the cathedral in Johannesburg, and told him of our plans, which were in no way political, but simply to continue research into the life of present-day missionaries. He asked us not to go. 'It's not your skin I'm worried about' (although *we* were worried enough about that) he told us bluntly. 'It's the work of the people you visit which will suffer. Things are much tougher than when you were last here. Even an innocent visit will be construed wrongly. I have worked here for many years, and I am not saying I would never speak out. But if the Church ever has a show-down with the government it should be on ground of our own choosing. We should not be dragged in by the accidents of visiting journalists.'

These were not the words of a coward. Within weeks the film *The Dumping Grounds* appeared on British television. In this film several missionary hospitals gave assistance to the producers in exposing the terrible hardships of Africans endorsed out to barren land in the open veld.

Although it was a disappointment, we felt it right to respect these wishes. So instead of visiting missionaries in South Africa we interviewed several back in Britain who were able to speak freely.

The pressures on a missionary who decides to work in present-day South Africa throw up most of the dilemmas of compromise. Like Alice in Wonderland, of course, the issues are back to front with the rest of Africa, but this does not matter to the question we want to look at: how a man under pressure of conscience reacts; and how in a complicated racial situation he sorts out the right relationship and the right path to follow as an expatriate, a Christian and a white.

Richard is also particularly interested in these issues in the South African context because in 1964 he went to South Africa with the deliberate intention of working within the system to bring change. He had accepted the job as General Manager of a relief organization and in it learnt something of trying to work within a system he despised. To begin with all your friends in England write you off. The inevitable conclusion is that you have betrayed any honesty towards Africans and the racial issue. The South African authorities, for their part, make no such assumption; Richard was tailed within four days of arriving in the country.

He had no conceivable political history that could interest them; except that he worked for Oxfam, and went to see the Oxfam-backed feeding scheme for drought relief in the Northern Transvaal.

The missionary he had gone to see subsequently told him that the Security Police visited him the day after and asked 'What was Mr. Exley doing here yesterday?' Not 'Who was that strange white man?' or 'Who was that Englishman?' It was all a bit chilling, which no doubt it was meant to be. From then on you realized that as *they* probably knew which cereals you had for breakfast you might as well plan your life accordingly.

From the start, you obey the law, you conform. You get off the plane at Jan Smuts Airport, Johannesburg, you come through immigration, and you write 'white' in the appropriate little box on the forms. You could of course make your stand for principle at this first barrier, if you chose. Richard dutifully wrote 'white' and entered the country. Then he wanted to go to the toilet. He walked over and faced obstacle two: the choice of white and black loos. He could, of course, have gone through the one marked 'non-white' and been escorted back to the plane as a trouble-maker within the first ten minutes. And so the subtleties of South African life began.

The real cleverness of the South African system is that it puts the onus of being a trouble-maker on you. You have to make the first move. All is peace and calm. There is no overt violence; no flailing truncheons; no vizored riot police. This has, of course, been achieved by a complete willingness to use the physical and legal Sharpevilles.

What, you may ask, is the point of carrying on in such circumstances? The answer to that one is a whole credo. You either believe human beings can get totally beyond the pale, or you don't.

The two political possibilities are for violent overthrow or change. But whichever happens, good men need to be around. This is the old liberal, humanitarian line, of course. It's not all that fashionable today, mainly because it is so often used and abused by those who would never stick their little toe out. The role of the Quakers in between-the-wars Germany was impressive in this way. Their integrity in giving relief to Germans immediately following the 'Hang the Kaiser' hate of 1918 earned them the enduring respect even of the SS. They did not, of course, stave off the inevitable; but the Quaker office in Berlin, under Corder Catchpool did save the lives of dozens of Jewish leaders on whose behalf they interceded. Individuals counted. More individuals thinking and acting likewise would count more.

Father William Burridge of the Catholic White Fathers explained to us that while they had withdrawn all the White Fathers from Mozambique (which has a strong racialist policy) they still felt they had work to do in South Africa. Both whites and blacks attend the different churches and the churches have managed to make brave stands on racial issues. Idealistically they've been the strongest opposition to government policy. If it wasn't for the continual pressure of the churches and other small brave groups the white Nationalist government would have a walkover. And missionaries have had extra freedom to speak out because their punishment is deportation and not house arrest or the other serious forms of punishment that the indigenous clergy face. But every missionary has to face the issues of compromise. You *have* to compromise if you go to South Africa or any other unjust situation. The only point for discussion becomes: when do you speak out and when do you keep quiet? And perhaps ultimately: when do you leave as a final protest?

*   *   *

We spoke to Rev. Parry Okeden, who had gone from this country to work in the Northern Transvaal in 1961. He had been one of the missionaries administering the Oxfam/Kupugani drought relief effort, so we had met before.

He had a tough time. He arrived to take over the supervision of work amongst a group of African Anglican churches. Potgietersrus is a predominantly Afrikaans community, with few white Anglicans. The maximum attendance at the white church was sixty or seventy on Christmas Day. Four times a year he used to hold multi-racial meetings. 'There were four whites who used to come: an accountant and his wife, a man who came from Botswana, a lady who didn't like the multi-racialism a bit but did it because it was right, and myself.'

He often discussed with people in South Africa whether there was a point in people coming out from the UK. 'My own feeling was that it was of value because clergymen could walk through the colour bar and have a fairly ordinary relationship.' Putting it no higher, 'you are probably the only people in the town who've been to tea with Africans'. You can also ask people back to your own house. The only other whites he saw in African areas were the Roman Catholic priest and government officials. 'I did have a real relationship with the Bantu Affairs Commissioner, Mr. Venter. He was quite brave. He would come to meetings and he would say "Whatever the Government says, there *is* drought."

Then whenever I went to see him he always spent the first three-quarters of an hour defending the government. We had a love-hate relationship. It was quite funny, really. From England you don't see that all white people in South Africa aren't bastards. They're nice in exactly the same proportions as here.'

Okeden, too, had his pressures. He was called a 'hyena in the making' by the Inspector of Education; he had visits from the Security Police, stones hurled on his roof, accusations that he was running the relief scheme for private gain. 'The worst thing was to walk through the town and think "God, how people hate me".'

How far can a man like Parry Okeden really go? He is a quietly spoken person; undramatic. See him in his vicarage in Oxford and he looks every bit the part. And yet in South Africa he is called a hyena. It isn't a matter of being scared of being thrown out. In his case he was the lynch pin around which a vital programme of child-feeding centred. If he went, children died. The thought of kwashiorkor and mirasmus victims in the hospitals is a stronger pressure than the personal implications of a one-way ticket.

'Often we had this feeling,' Parry told us. 'Should we protest or should we let it go this time because it's not important enough? I think on the whole I was too chicken. But one didn't know whether one was right or just being chicken.'

He did stick his neck out. He wrote passionate letters about the drought distress to the press. He took a couple of reporters around—one of the things that most annoys the authorities. Reporters are not allowed into the African reserves without permits; but on this occasion Venter said, 'take them round. I don't know about it.'

Then the authorities told Okeden's relief committee to stop distributing food, so he got the church to do it. Then they wrote and told the church to stop. 'Then I just did it myself and made sure no one else was involved. You have to say to yourself "It's not me who's mad." '

'Once I took a woman to a bank to help her. There was no notice segregating counters, but it was custom. I went in with her to the non-white teller. All the typewriters stopped. I felt I was commiting some awful social gaffe.'

He faced this sort of thing on all sorts of occasions. 'Over and over again when I was travelling with Africans we would stop by the side of the road to have something to eat and see people nearly drive into a tree trying to turn round and see. There was electricity in the air when white parishioners walked into your house when you were having black friends to tea. The worst thing was meeting a (black) friend in the street and not knowing whether to shake hands: if you did he might be in trouble; if you didn't he might be insulted. We once had a service in a hut near the border. Someone must have spotted the strange car and reported us because three policemen dashed in, two white and one black. I knew the black one very well: should I shake hands with none or all? In the event I shook hands with all of them. Afterwards the black man told me he said to the white policemen words to the effect: "Well, he's a bit funny that way." '

*   *   *

Dr. John Davies is one of those who decided that, for him, the right course was to leave South Africa. He, too, tried to run his parish as one unit. 'On one occasion I had 40 African and 4 white candidates for confirmation. The question was should we bring the blacks to the white church in town, which would be big enough; or should we take them to the biggest African church in the location. The answer, to me, was the latter. So I went to each household and explained that we were having the service in the location. In each case I saw one parent and each said "all right". In the next three or four days I got furious replies from the spouses I had not seen: "We couldn't possibly do this because the children would have to go back to school and say they were confirmed in the African location. They would face the question: 'What are you becoming—a kaffir?' " We compromised and had it at our house thirty miles away.'

Dr. Davies did not find it easy. 'You come from outside. You are free of this racial thing. But you have to bear in mind the whites are victims of their environment. As a Christian, our Lord's attitude is not to blame people for things outside their control—the woman taken in adultery, for example.'

Davies echoed all of Okeden's arguments about pressure: 'You don't know how far to go in case you get chopped—not thrown out, but the work spoiled in some way. If I get notorious as a student chaplain, will I be able to minister to a middle of the road student who is not committed? South Africa teaches you that Christianity is not a matter of principles but a response to an immediate situation, a situation where you become unpredictable and unreliable. Because you are trying to care for people and because the situation shifts rapidly you and your responsibilities alter. I am reminded of the position of the Confessing Church in Nazi Germany in the 'thirties saying it was always in opposition; the crunch was to decide the immediate thing for the here and now. Christians have talked a hell of a lot about principles—as if it was a matter of taking a whole lot of principles on a piece of paper and applying them.'

Davies believed that Jung was on to something very important when he said that 'Creative living begins on the yonder side of convention'. One cannot avoid being smeared by the mess. A real part of the Christian purpose was to live where there were no ideal courses.

There is a tremendous difference between this attitude and the attitude of any simple revolutionary, who must divide into right and wrong, and overthrow the wrong. Christians we met in South Africa refused to be totally condemning of human beings. As the Quakers would perhaps put it, they were 'searching for that of God in every man'. In this way lay the only real progress, the only real change in men's hearts. All other change was superficial. Davies recognized that peoples' real happiness cannot be manipulated economically. 'This is childishness. But it is desparately bad for people to be exercising unbridled power. The people who suffer most from injustice are those who impose it.'

Take a walk along Eloff Street, Johannesburg, and measure human happiness by its more obvious sign—laughter, conviviality and smiles. I will lay a bet with anyone that there are more smiles per mile on the black faces than there are on the white. And this is not to be Afrophile. The reason is bound up with the culture. The European is tight up with sexual frustration, tight up with worries about his money, tight up with worries about the black man whom he so barely understands. Dr. Davies said that he was reminded of a very inconspicuous priest, 'who had never said boo to a goose', who said to him: 'The problem you'll find here is dishonesty, particularly in marriage. People who adopt such a basically dishonest attitude racially must become dishonest in marriage.' (There were more whites divorced than married in Johannesburg in 1970.)

Dr. Davies would not go out to South Africa again: in principle he would now think it wrong to do so; but he would not think it right to dictate to others who thought otherwise. He would think it wrong to go out again not because of the difficulties of compromising, but because of the need for the growth of a comparable black power in relation to the white. 'Unless there is something like parity in power, talk about reconciliation is premature. I want the ordinary churches to be available for reconciliation and I don't think they're going to be unless we make a leadership vacuum.'

Davies felt that he had to get out to make way for more militant black church leadership. And the crunch issue for him was whether or not to take citizenship. 'I felt very deeply wrong being on the fringe, not really sharing their situation. If you're born in it you can't evade it. I had the option.' He was very torn. He nearly applied for citizenship, he got the papers, but drew back mainly because of his children—'One had to face the fact that my niche in South Africa was not worth the cost to my children.'

CHAPTER EIGHT

Lesotho and Botswana

On, then, to Lesotho and Botswana. These were the last two countries in Africa where we travelled extensively meeting missionaries. By this time there was perhaps a feeling that we had seen it all. What could be new to write about in yet more hospitals, schools, aid projects? This chapter is given over to exceptions; to the people who for one reason or another defy any attempt to slot them into categories. There were five such people or groups; three in Lesotho and two in Botswana. These plus a 'plane crash and riding on horseback through the Lesotho mountains safely ensured the absence of boredom.

Lesotho is a strange country, almost all of it mountainous, with some of the mountains up to 10,000 feet and more; the only exception is a small strip of fertile plain along the Orange River, where many of the Masuto farmers live. In a way it is like Wales without the factories of the south, but much more isolated and less developed. The country is poor. It has no resources except a few diamonds in the east and water, which all flows out to South Africa, the country which surrounds and makes an island of the tiny nation. There is little or no industry. Manufactured goods are imported from South Africa. The main occupation is *sub*-subsistence farming, with maize and wood as the staples. Ironically, even the traditional colourful blankets of the Masuto mountain horsemen are made from wool woven and dyed in South Africa.

It is a completely pastoral and rural society. And in such a society, uncluttered by the kind of urban problems found in Kenya, missionaries have played a more clear and evident role than perhaps in any other country in Africa.

*   *   *

ANNE BENT (page 105ff) photographed in a South London Street, near Church Missionary Society headquarters. She looks very much an ordinary woman in a crowd: certainly it would be hard to type her as a 'missionary': and still harder to imagine her as the stoic heroine who ran the largest hospital in war torn 'Biafra'.

STEPHEN CARR is an agricultural missionary. He turned down a job at £14,000 a year, tax free. He is brilliant, yet stays in a backwater. 'All your managerial ability is moving out of the grass-roots level, developing plans which may be perfectly sound, but which have no hope of fulfilment.'

above. But when Carr built his house, he spurned plans for a European-style bungalow costing £5,000. No-one he said, could ever expect to live like that in that area: so why should he. Instead, he built himself an attractive mud, wattle and thatch bungalow with materials from the forest – at a cost of £140. See story pages 19ff.

right. Young tea seedlings at Bunyoro, Uganda. Carr has served as a missionary in Nigeria, Sudan and Uganda. At Bunyoro, he carved a tea estate from virgin forest and provided a prosperous livelihood to unemployed school leavers. Characteristically, when he bought his first tea plant, he paid one of the highest prices ever paid in Uganda. Only the best would do.

BROTHER WILLIAM. He is not exactly the image of the monk. 'We're only ordinary people and we can only communicate in terms of our own experience. . . Communication only starts by being friends and builds up like that. I don't think there's any question of coming Bible thumping and thousands of people flocking after you. It's nothing like that.' (Page 90ff)

above:
GORDON MARSHALL is a missionary pilot. He flies with the 'Missionary Aviation Fellowship', an organization that has its own fleet of light aircraft ferrying missionary personnel to the remoter parts of the globe. He is an ex-South African Defence force pilot, and was our guide on many East African trips.

right:
MISSIONARY WIVES
'I wish people would see me as normal' one of the young wives said to us. They told us of the pressures to conform, to be the 'godly examples' of the Book of Common Prayer. (See page 128ff)

FATHER RICHARD was one of the few missionaries who still worked as a local parish priest, in a quiet backwater of Tanzania. 'I don't ever want to go back to England,' he says. Unlike the modern 'contract-missionary' out for a short spell as a specialist, he has adopted the life-style of his parishioners, lives in a mud hut, and sleeps on a hand-made bed. 'We came out to live like Africans,' he says. (See page 72ff)

above:
JOHN MOCKFORD, in total contrast, came out to serve the new élite of the cities: an élite that is rapidly moving away from Christianity. The Mockford family live in a modern bungalow, 'the poor paupers of the managing directors up the hill and the rich uncles of the Africans down below'. (See story page 45ff)

right:
PIPPA GAYE is another 'missionary character'. Discharged from the war with a weak heart, she became a missionary at 40. Now she runs a hospital in a remote Botswana village — without a doctor. Back home on leave, she attended a Landrover course so that she could be her own mechanic, and did a two-year course in radiography in nine days.

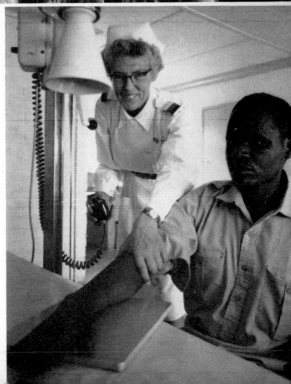

above:
ROBERT AND JILL DE
BERRY (See page 148) are
undergoing training. The dress is
casual. They sport an old Morris
Minor, decorated with stick-on
flowers. They are full of fun, with
scant respect for the trappings of
the established church. 'The biggest test of my faith,' says Robert,
'is not getting on with unbelievers,
so much as getting on with my
fellow clergy.'

right:
KEVIN AND PENNY
LAWES were fashionably dressed. Penny had, we heard, caused
something of a sensation the previous summer when she appeared
in flame red hotpants. (See page
150 ff) 'I think we are going to
shock a few people. We are not
of the same world as the old
missionaries and even of some of
the younger ones.'

One of our strongest memories of Lesotho is of a visit to Mantsonyane, a mission station at the end of the 'Mountain Road'—a
twisting, hairpin-bend track, impassable in wet weather, that
winds for 52 miles into the mountains. The road had lost two
vehicles over the edge that month. We had come to see two
things: the functioning of one of the newer hospitals in the heart
of the country and an Anglican brother and priest who lived
high on a mountainside in an old-style 'mission station', looking
after the little mountain churches and schools in the vicinity of
the hospital.

The hospital at Mantsonyane had perhaps taken some strides
into the future by appointing a Jewish doctor as medical superintendent. This in many ways un-missionary type act had, unfortu-
nately, led to disaster, with a severe difference of opinion between
the doctor and the hospital board back in Maseru. Dr. Cohen,
young, bearded, and bitter, disliked the amount of flag-sticking
going on amongst the mission societies. He maintained that the
number of patients seen by his particular hospital certainly did
not justify a fully fledged hospital staff and doctor. He reckoned
that one doctor travelling by land-rover could have serviced the
four hospitals within 30 miles of Mantsonyane. From a Christian
proselytization point of view there may be a need for the four
hospitals. Medically, they would do better to combine. Certainly
his was one of the quietest hospitals we had seen.

The trouble with logical thinking like Dr. Cohen's is that
missionary work isn't logical. If it was, the people who give
money to establish the hospitals would have spent their money
on an extra room for their own house, or a holiday in the South
of France. Giving is a very illogical act. And people who give
tend to be partisan. One suspects that the trouble with Dr.
Cohen's thesis is that if one did rationalize the medical services
and amalgamate the four hospitals, there might not be enough
support to sustain even one of them.

We tried not to let ourselves be drawn into this particular
argument. The people at the hospital, and the goings on were
enough to keep us occupied. We stayed up late the first evening
with a communal supper, feeling very tried after a gruelling day.
Around nine o'clock Matron had to leave us to go to a woman
in final stages of labour. 'Do you want to come along and watch
a birth?' she asked Helen. 'I'm just going along for the final

G

stage, it won't be long now.' Helen went and this is her description of what followed:

Old hands may smile at my naïvety; this was quite some experience for me. I expected some grunting, and so on; I knew that African women do not usually scream. And at first it was nice and rather sweet: there, neatly laid out, was a hand-knitted blanket all the way from England. Mother, or almost mother, was smiling and everyone was cheerful.

About six hours later we were still there, and it was pretty gory. I was exhausted. The heat was stifling. The lights had gone out. I remember at one stage thrusting the gas lamp I was holding into Matron's hands and rushing out into the cool corridor. I was wet through with sweat and lay on the cold floor.

After that I didn't have time to faint. 'Pull the leg up with your right shoulder there. Move the lamp over. Pass that clean cloth.' The worst bit was cutting the flesh to let the head through. There was a spurt of blood. I couldn't faint. I wouldn't have dared. Matron was totally in command. She had brought me along as a tourist. Now she needed every bit of help she could get. She had the command of a sergeant major. This was not the timid little bird-like person I had been talking to at the party. This was the woman, who through sheer tension in her body and voice could command total attention and obedience.

The crisis continued. When the baby arrived, we simply could not get him to breathe. We wrapped up a hot water bottle to try to keep him warm. 'Pump', Matron commanded as I used a tube to get his lungs and nose clear. 'More oxygen.' My foot ached with the foot pump. 'Pump harder.' A few minutes beyond normal survival time, he breathed. It was, Matron admitted, a terrible birth.

Around 3 a.m. I crawled back to bed, with some idea what staff in a place like this take in their stride. Matron was up on duty at 6 a.m. I slept till noon.

*   *   *

The next day we walked across one of the deep valleys to go to Brother William's place. To get there you go down, down, down a steep and twisting path to a sweeping river, roll your trousers up and wade through when the river is not in flood. Horsemen overtake with huge grins. Then you turn off into a side valley, up a twisting road that is, theoretically, passable to a land-rover. For all our land-rover experience I wouldn't have liked to negotiate this one with 3-feet dongas and a nice drop to the side. Up a tiny winding track, with boulders and storm drains to stop you being swept off, up to a tiny hamlet of stone and thatch huts, a bit of barbed wire, some scrawny goats, and laughter and music. Miles from the nearest road. And here, perched on the hillside, Brother William had his home.

A more unlikely Brother would be hard to imagine. I suppose I always think of the monastic orders as intellectual, aesthetic, reading St. Thomas Aquinas or something all day. Brother William was utterly, but utterly, down to earth. For a start he didn't wear robes. Like Stephen Carr, he had dirty knees, and was totally informal. He swore if he felt like it. The first time we saw him he was covered in grease mending a car, with a great shock of untidy hair on top and a big grin he looked more like Adam Faith than a monk. But devotion, yes, he had a brand of his own. As we went out in the evening for a stroll he greeted all the youngsters around who depended on the mission for their education. He was more of a Masutho, than he was British. His hesitance with us disappeared as he mixed with the local people. You could see it in the ever so simple way the home was furnished. There were soft, floppy easy chairs, a few favourite books, a comfortable tea pot, fags on the table. What sort of man becomes a monk these days? Could he tell us why? Does he really get across with his message? We were very curious.

His background was working class; he started life in a factory; and he had a broad drawl of an accent. No blinding act of conversion drove him to his vocation. 'I think my decisions were made for me in one sense. Most of us have never had a conversion. Perhaps we have just been brought up this way. We've been conditioned to this way of life within the Church of England and when it comes to making a decision we're somewhat biased to start with. But I think we all have our own way.' He admits communication about matters like this is difficult. 'We're only ordinary people and we can only communicate in terms of our own experience. Obviously some people in the outside world, indeed outside the Church, are able to give lucid and clear descrip-

tions of what they're doing and why. But if you ask me, I can't.
I couldn't give a clear description of why I joined the community in the first place.

'Really you know, communication only starts by being friends
and builds up like that. I don't think there's any question of
coming round Bible thumping and thousands of people flocking
after you. It's nothing like that.'

Brother William was not a man of decision. But his easy going
slow-speaking diffident manner was convincing in its own way.
He had sunk completely into African ways. On one occasion
he turned and spoke to us, without thinking, in Sesotho. We felt
we would probably have got a much better interview in fact if
we could have conducted the conversation in Sesotho rather than
English. He rarely left the village. His pocket money from the
community ran to cigarettes or a trip to Maseru occasionally.
'And what can you do when you get to Maseru?'

Brother William and Father David, the priest he shared the
house with, had made this out-of-the-way spot their life. Every
day one or other of them rode miles across the hills to take Mass,
do a christening or see a catechist. Unproductive? Yes, but
strangely moving in our fast, dynamic nineteen-seventies.

One day we rode out from Mantsonyane on horseback, four
hours each way to visit a tiny primary school. This was the most
painful experience we had as we can't ride. We went there on
examination day, and the invigilator we talked to had walked
there that morning, several hours across the hills; he would walk
back in the evening. If we say that we stumbled and climbed
and descended three ravines, each more than a thousand feet deep,
then we have conveyed some idea of the lot of a schoolteacher
in those parts.

The day was fine enough to give a very clear idea of the
country. All you could see on both sides were steep hills tortuously
winding rivers, and occasionally, scratched on to a contoured
hill, a small plot of maize. Most places are inaccessible even to a
land-rover. In a few places there are airstrips, but for the rest it is
horseback and Shanks's pony.

The school was a cluster of buildings; sturdy stone-built little
classrooms, rather like you would imagine in a remote Welsh
or highland village. When there is no road, and the nearest
landrover point is four hours away by horse, the calm normality

of the teaching day is the surprise. Desks, chalk, books, all went on as surely as if distance and remoteness was no problem at all. To be sure there were problems. History centred around John Knox. Geography was of English towns. There was a chronic shortage of teaching aids, and no maps. But the very existence of the school, when every stick and rafter had been carried, was an achievement. When we had listened to the haunting singing of the children, we watched them wind away down the paths over the hills, off to distant kraals.

★   ★   ★

Our next port of call in Lesotho was to the Scott Hospital at Morija. This was run with the support of the Paris Evangelical Society and in terms of sheer service to people in need it must stand as the most impressive hospital we visited.

We were met by Dr. N. D. Abbey, one of the three doctors. He took us on a quick tour of the hospital, and this showed just how much can be squeezed out of human beings. In the previous year the three doctors had seen 76,861 out-patients, admitted 3,431 bed-patients, performed 3,191 minor operations and 346 major operations and delivered 776 babies, as well as handling epidemics of diphtheria, anthrax and typhoid.

The hospital has no administrative back-up to support it, as in Britain. And when you consider that the average British family doctor has 2,478 patients on his list, these figures assume their real meaning. No one in Lesotho comes complaining of depression or 'flu.

To achieve this sort of work, of course, some extras have to go. The doctors perform about 100 caesarian sections a year, and do almost all of them under spinal anaesthetics, with the patients wide awake. This way, they need only one doctor present at a time. There is only one doctor to 40,000 people in Lesotho, and only one anaesthetist in the whole country.

Pressure on bed space is terrific. 'We don't admit pneumonia cases as long as they can breathe. We couldn't *think* of doing so. And if we are certain someone is going to die, we can't admit them. We would have no trouble filling our beds twice over.' As it is, there are patients lying under the beds on mattresses,

and lying on matresses in the corridors; there are two and more
to a cot in the children's wards.

We walked round the kitchens. They were not the stainless
steel wonders you expect. They were grimy with smoke; old;
battered. Cockroaches skudded across the floors. 'Don't worry,'
Dr. Abbey assured us, 'Cockroaches are not known to carry
disease.' On one occasion, he told us, they had a particularly
portly cook; the floorboards were old, and the cook fell straight
through. The hospital's priorities are elsewhere. They want a
burns unit—they get terrible burns from the villagers' primitive stoves. They need a children's ward, two new general
wings, and a nurses' quarters to enable them to do higher training.

Just sometimes when you write about a place like Scott Hospital
at Morija, you wish that some reader who really had the money
would up and pack his bags and go and see for himself, and then
give them one of the things they so badly need. I can't think how
anyone could get more happiness from giving away a few
thousand.

Sometimes people *are* generous. But sometimes human mean-
ness hurts. Dr. Abbey told us that he tries not to get too personally
involved with too many of the patients: he couldn't survive if
he did. But sometimes it's inevitable. And it must be pretty
galling when he writes, as he did in one instance, to a personal
friend who has a $100,000 apartment asking him for $150 for
one particular child to go to school, only to get a 'No'.

As a person, Dr. Abbey is memorable. He has a bustling,
thrusting energy. He was invigoratingly cheerful to all he met,
a sort of living Dale Carnegie without the false trying. Wherever
he goes round the hospital, he makes sure that one senior nurse
or medical aid is with him. There can never be enough doctors
in the foreseeable future, Dr. Abbey believes, so he should make
sure that someone is with him at all times to soak up whatever
knowledge he can pass on. 'Each one teach one' is his motto.
He recalls that as late as the beginning of the twentieth century
in the country where he was trained, Canada, an apprentice
followed a doctor around for a year until he thought he knew
the business, and then struck off on his own, put up his plaque
and called himself doctor. Something similar would be useful in
developing countries, Abbey believes.

He has a happy relationship with the African staff. 'I don't have to be on my guard because they're judging me or because they will tell other people what you do.'

One of the other three doctors at Morija, Dr. Chris de Reynier, told us something of some of the kinds of problems the patients of the hospital faced outside the hospital. She instanced the transport problems by telling the story of a time when she was staying in the mountains with a minister. 'At 11 a.m. a messenger came to say that the wife of an evangelist had broken her leg "Would I go?" I was asked. I went. We couldn't get horses right away so we walked for two hours. The woman had a very bad fracture. I gave her morphia and antibiotics and got her on a stretcher, then I went back to the river to check that the river man would stay on. The minister yelled and yelled. No answer. Then a voice came back: "Tomorrow". We couldn't cross the Orange. We stayed in a village and she died during the night. But even if we had got across the Orange we would have had a long, long journey. In these parts, when people know it's too bad they just don't even attempt to get to hospital.'

Things are changing here. Ten years ago you would see forty or fifty horses tethered outside the hospital. Now the majority come by bus, at least in the lowland areas. Health has improved. 'We used to see a lot of kwashiorkor (malnutrition), now we call the nurses to see it. People are coming to hospital sooner.'

Poignantly, one of the reasons why Scott Hospital is so crowded is because it is so good. There is little doubt, from what we could see, that the services were streets ahead of those provided in the few government hospitals. 'They like the attitude of personal concern here. They are treated as individuals. The government hospitals run out of drugs.' Many other hospitals were without doctors altogether. Most of the country's 30 doctors are concentrated in the one small town of Maseru. Political disturbances lost at least three good Masuto doctors who were forced to leave the country.

Scott Hospital, although impressive, is an example of one of the big problems facing the missionary societies. When they established 'mission stations', taught needy people to read and write, and ministered to their medical needs (hoping in the process to get something of their Christian convictions across) they had a quite clear function. The great missionary institutions that have

sprung up around the world—the fine hospitals and schools—
are a bricks and mortar testimony to this.

But all over Africa, these institutions are being rapidly phased
out, and are being handed over to the new African governments.
The missionary societies themselves welcome this, believing that
more and more Christians will come to serve in the new secular
hospitals. In many ways one can see they are right—in theory.
But when you visit somewhere like Scott Hospital, you can't
help but have a nostalgia for independent institutions at their
finest. The dedication is so obvious. There are no arbitrary job
distinctions. If something needs doing it is done.

Scott Hospital—and that, if one is honest, means the three
expatriate doctors—soldiers on on its own. The fledgling Lesotho
Evangelical Church clearly can't underwrite £30,000 as did the
Paris Evangelical Society. 'This hospital lives on faith. We have
no board or anything behind us', Dr. de Reynier told us. They
earn every penny of their operating costs on the fees they have
to charge; a flat 3s. a day per patient. They rely on people like
Oxfam for capital costs of new buildings. But they find it almost
impossible to plan intelligently into the future. If the effectiveness
of government hospitals increased for instance, the number of
their patients might go down, but should they go on planning
on the basis of someone else's inadequacy? There is no answer.
So they work from day to day. Which makes the whole story
even more incredible.

*   *   *

And so to Botswana.

In Botswana we visited a Dutch Reformed mission hospital,
and this was intriguing in itself. We were curious to see how a
church which endorsed the tyranny of apartheid in South Africa
would preach the love of Christ 30 miles away in an independent
multi-racial country.

We were glad to arrive at the hospital, any hospital. Our eldest
son, Lincoln, was down with a severe throat infection and fever,
picked up soon after we left. We were doubly anxious hearing
the word 'diphtheria'. But all was well, and we were met by a
bustling grey-haired, white-coated old lady who introduced
herself as Mrs. Teichler. She took immediate matronly charge,

bundled the children into bed, sat down, made tea, and organized. A little later Dr. Teichler came on the scene. He was lanky, shy, distinctly professorial looking.

They showed us round the hospital, strangely situated amidst a kopje of rocks, and in the evening we sat down to try to get to know the Teichlers. We realized fairly quickly that we would have to cast aside any preconceptions about the Dutch Reformed Church, and indeed about our hosts. We had heard a lot of criticism in the village of Mochudi nearby. According to some of the Peace Corps volunteers the hospital was very self-contained. 'The South African Afrikaans group do not associate with the Setswana . . . they are less friendly than the Catholics.' Some of the Setswana, too, were bitter. 'The missionaries are like men in a prison—the Peace Corps men are more friendly', one told us, 'the missionaries think we are not quite human.'

The Teichlers had been very hurt by these and other criticisms levelled at them by the young brood of international volunteers in the village. In certain ways, they certainly were authoritarian and old fashioned in attitude. They will, for example, give out "the pill" only to married mothers going on teachers training or to an epileptic mother with seven children.

'We have too much to do. We don't want to get involved. It is beyond our strength and beyond our principles. Are we to encourage promiscuity? At school, once a girl is pregnant she is thrown out. It's the same here. It's not that we condemn them. But once their mind is on sex things they don't concentrate on their studies. Also, pills are expensive, even if we could get them from WHO.'

On our way through the wards we glanced at the latest pages in the register of births. On one page 5 out of 16 mothers were married. On the other 4 out of 12. The pill would certainly have cut down their work.

The Teichlers tended to resent the sexual licence of the volunteers, and the way they mixed with the local girls. 'Dancing in petticoats doesn't appeal to us. We haven't got time to throw parties and have social life for them.' The word 'them' for Africans kept recurring in conversation. And you could see a mile off that mission work to the Teichlers was a question of loving, dutiful service, something basically done for and to a people. The Teichlers and the volunteers were a generation and a half apart. Some of the volunteers knew and respected the Teichlers, but for others everything was judged on 'communication', the great nineteen-seventies OK word. The volunteers were good at communication. But as we came to know the Teichlers, we began to think they would still be there serving in their slightly stiff way long after the volunteers have ceased communicating.

The Teichlers' story is an epic in perserverance. Dr. Teichler and his wife are German and started missionary work in the nineteen-thirties in Tanganyika. They had 8 children, and were interned in a concentration camp by the British throughout the second world war.

They had come to Mochudi at the end of their lives, but they have not stopped. At fifty-three Mrs. Teichler decided that now the children were off her hands she would train as a midwife. Dr. Teichler decided at sixty-one that he could no longer stand the number of people going blind with preventable blindness. So he packed his bags and went off to Moorfields in London to become an eye specialist. Now he's the only one in Botswana. Several of their children are now missionaries in South Africa.

On our second evening with the Teichlers, Richard went along to witness an eye operation for the removal of a cataract. In that hot theatre, surrounded by a qualified African nursing staff, there was somthing strangely moving about the old doctor. He was long past the age when most surgeons give up. White strands of hair stuck out from under his theatre cap. And delicately, ever so delicately, he slit the eye, gently, ever so gently, prised out the opaque and damaged lens, then stitched up the eye again with minutely fine stitches.

Later in the evening, watching a reddened and setting sun from his veranda, we caught a glimpse of Dr. Teichler quietly, almost unobtrusively, reading from his Bible. He sat there a long time, deep in contemplation.

This was old-time mission work; one couldn't help but think of Dr. Teichler as a sort of unknown Schweitzer.

Mrs. Teichler kept her own little museum—odd seed pods, beadwork bushmen instruments, odd bones—all very dusty. The whole house was big and shambolic and really lived in. Stuffed under every bed were papers, journals, textbooks. There were lampshades of dried leaves made by the children. Fossils, shells, animal skulls. More than most houses you visit, this was a home. We felt strangely protective and sympathetic to the Teichlers. To the young volunteers they were incredibly old fashioned. They *were*—but they had served for forty years. Hindsight is terribly easy. These people were from the old world —they were still terribly German with all that is strongly cultural, with all that we think too authoritarian. They were like a caricature of the old Germany. They had not for forty years read the OK books. They had no modern attitudes. All their 8 children had played musical instruments with 'Vader' leading. It could almost have been out of an old movie. You cannot condemn people for being of their generation and not having the new attitudes which make modern missionaries less arrogant, less certain that civilization has all the answers.

We liked the Teichlers, they were kind to us despite the fact that we were 'journalists'—dreaded by the Dutch Reformed in case we would write an exposé. They didn't trust us. Well, the morals were stiff, the methods a bit dusty, the doctor had his own separate world. But 'till their death and many of their children's deaths the Teichlers will still be there or somewhere, doing a fine job. If they get thrown out for being Afrikaans they'll go to South West Africa. I can still see Papa Teichler badgering a very agitated Frau Teichler with the idea that Mochudi was getting too busy and modern and they really ought to go off and start a new clinic in the desert; somewhere nice and remote.

*　　*　　*

The last place we stayed at in Botswana was in some ways one of the most remote; this was St. Peter's Mission Hospital Mmadinare.

There are very few places in the world today that are really remote, but Mmadinare comes pretty near to it.

We approached from Serowe, the last village of any size. We drove north along a hundred miles of the hot dusty main highway that runs north–south through Botswana. The road is perhaps 150 feet wide, straight as a die, firm in places, rutted in others. There is no tar. You see a car, lorry, pedestrian or herd of cattle perhaps every ten miles. It is incredibly hot, over 100°F, and very dry with it, with all the windows of the car open, liberal supplies of Coke, and ample petrol, you pray that your modern miracle, the car, gets from A to B. You have no wish to sit by the road and wait for a breakdown truck to come 150 miles or more. After 100 miles, you turn off at a two-shop, one-garage village and strike off along a minor dirt road. If there were signposts, they have gone. You ask someone the way. 'Turn left after a mile,' he says. Five miles goes by and no left turn appears. Then a left turn with no sign—do you go? And so on. For 35 questioning miles we drove through scrub trees of fairly presentable size. Everyone thinks of Botswana and the Kalahari as desert. But savannah and drought-resistant thorn trees would be more accurate in the eastern part. In the 35 miles we saw no vehicle or human. Then, with a rising apprehension as to where we were, we came across the village. This is quite unlike anything in Europe. Some thousands of families live in clusters of huts scattered haphazardly over several square miles. Their goats and chickens run around over unplanned and generous common land in all directions. Something, perhaps, like the villages of England before twentieth-century infillers made every square foot into money.

Past the odd shop, a once-a-week Barclays Bank, and a petrol station—the minimum status points for entry into the twentieth century—and on to the hospital. And it is then, at the end of 135 miles of dust, scrub and loneliness that you realize what an amazing monument to determination and resolution these mission hospitals are. Neat modern buildings—not by any stretch of the imagination lavish, but white washed, efficient; surrounded by flowers. We had seen it many times before. But it always came with a glow of surprise. It is good to realize you have shelter.

There is no doctor here, only Pippa Gaye. But she is character enough. We didn't intend to write up missionaries as a series of heroic characters. But characters they are, and some superlatives are going to be inevitable in any realistic write-up of Pippa Gaye. She is very tall, gangley, thin, greying and very, very resolute. She was only half expecting us, as we hadn't been able to confirm our arrival time after an initial letter some weeks back. She swallowed and counted ten. She set us down to cool drinks, then organized beds, and finally showed us round her outpost empire. As she went the rounds, she paced a determined thrusting stride. We had to half-run to keep up. She walked rather like a racy sports car driver and zoomed around the corners.

First the statistics, then the woman. Pippa Gaye runs a hospital which has had no doctor for six years. It is a 58-bed hospital, which has three out-clinics, with more beds at a place called Boboneng. In the course of a year she and her five African sisters see 34,709 out-patients, handle 565 maternity cases, 620 X-rays and 209 minor operations. She is the only white person in the village. She lives a quiet, reclusive life in her bungalow.

She told us about her life. 'It is difficult to say really why I became a missionary. I was discharged from the war with a weak heart.' (Shades of Stephen Carr with his weak lungs.) 'I looked after my parents and worked for seven years in Dorset helping old people. At forty I reached a crossroads. I had not married. I had no ties. I discussed this with my Vicar. I knew nothing of missions, but I knew the SPG was my place from the minute I went in. I had some problems. I had been out of training for nineteen years, and out of nursing fifteen years. I thought I could do any job rather than nursing.'

From that point she started through all the procedures. Six references, training at Selly Oak. 'The normal course was one or two years. I only did one term, when Dr. Veronica Threws came. "Well now, dear, I think it's time to do your midwifery, don't you?" Me, at my time of life! So I got the names and wrote off. Most places had an age limit of 40, or else would bar me because of my medical history. But for all my history I am in fact very healthy. So I cheated a bit. I got myself examined by a dear old fellow, and never got a stethoscope near my chest. I guessed we'd have a medical, so I got Veronica to write a letter. When my turn came, the doc asked what an old grey one was doing among all these young things. We got talking about the army. All he did was run his hand up and down my legs: "Long stringy kind. You'll be all right." In the event there were 12 recruits and I was the only one that never got sick.

'The midwifery training was at Deptford. It was grim but I loved it. Only two-thirds passed. You can't pick and choose your questions in the exam. It's no use saying "I can't answer an asphyxiated baby, I'll leave that one." Dr. Veronica booked my passage before the results. She asked me how long I needed to prepare myself and I said about two months. She made it eight weeks to the day.

'So in the beginning of 1962 I arrived at Gwelo in the middle of the night. It was raining, and I was met by an old diesel land-rover.

'I had no preconceived ideas of Africa, although I had been in West and North Africa during the war.' At this point she must have detected a look on Helen's face, for she went on 'Oh yes, you imagine army nurses as fiery dragons—like many people think of missionaries, plodding through the bush. But life in the army was under harder conditions than here. We lived in tents without baths for two-and-half years; we wore men's battledress and boots.' Then—with a grin—'It's an asset in living as a missionary. You know the mysteries of French drains, water shortages and improvisation.

'The last doctor left after I had been here three years, and I've been alone ever since. I'm glad of company, but I've learned to live on my own.' How does she cope with the fateful decisions she must inevitably take? 'You learn that it's no good tearing yourself apart. You learn to discipline yourself. You don't get anywhere by crying yourself to sleep. And you don't get hard by it. If you make an error of judgement, you've tried—and made a mistake. You've got to take ghastly decisions. You're three hours drive from Francistown, and sometimes in rain the road is unnavigable.'

Does she keep her cool under such situations? 'No. I know we're all supposed to be little angels, but when people bring burns cases three days later, or a gastroenteritis child within an hour of death my reaction is to lose my temper. But I come down to earth as quickly as I fly off it. I've been here seven years and I waver between optimism and pessimism. Take breast feeding, for instance. Bottle feeding has caught on. It's the in-thing to do, and it's absolutely exasperating because they can't manage it. Other people have a suck. The bottle rolls on the floor. There's no boiling. And because powdered milk is frightfully expensive they resort to unboiled cows' milk. Then bring the child in half dead. One mother came in with a week-old skeleton of a child. We got the breast milk stimulated again and I gave the mother a lecture. She said she didn't know she'd be made to breast feed, she might as well go home. But at the end of the week she got interested, and now she's done a lot of good spreading the good word.'

When she first arrived in Mmadinare, she says, she was 'very green'. 'One night a young boy of fifteen arrived and said, "Can you come; a woman has been in labour for two days?" So I decided to go. Three miles from here I got stuck in the sand of a river bed, so I walked. There I was, walking, walking, walking and I kept saying, "Where?" The reply was always, "It is not far." We walked for three hours. He never faltered. When we arrived at 10 p.m. the woman had delivered and was all right. They were very welcoming and all that, but after ten minutes I said I'd be on my way back. I'd worn my soles out by then. I wouldn't be so daft now. I was about forty-four when this took place. When I got back that night—it was a frightfully hot night—the night nurse had taken off her uniform and was just working in her operating gown. She giggled and clutched rather inefectually at her large bottom. I'd find it hard to settle in England now.'

Pippa Gaye may not be so green now, but she still turns out at all hours of the night. Only a few weeks before we had arrived a sixteen-year-old girl—who had been warned to come at the first sign of labour because she needed a caesar—came late, at 10 p.m. on a Sunday evening. Pippa drove through the night alone. 'Only 10 miles short of Francistown I was blinded by a car overtaking; I pulled up with a jerk and everything went dead I thought it must be electrical, so I opened up and the first thing I saw was the battery lying down broken off. I heaved it up, sat it in the cradle and re-did the terminals. Nothing. I kept thinking what can I do? Two and a half hours later I was still there. Then I thought: It must be that little wire that goes into the side. So out with the nail file and scissors. About 3 a.m. we arrived in Francistown.'

Then, with a smile: 'I don't usually go alone because everyone else gets steamed up. People get a bit bothered if I stay up all night.'

Pippa Gaye, as we said earlier, is a character. It seemed amazing to see a British woman so at home, so adaptable to an entirely different culture to which she is the only exception. Like the Teichlers, she had simply equipped herself for the job. If she was going to drive land-rovers through the night, she thought, she should be able to take them to pieces. So one home leave she went along to the land-rover works to take a maintenance course. She was, needless to say, the only woman there, let alone the only woman over forty. She inherited an X-ray machine at the hospital which no one knew how to use. So again, next time home she went along to Guys to do radiography, to be told it was a two-year course. She said 'I've got nine days'. Now she runs the X-ray machine at St. Peter's.

Pippa was the last missionary we met on our African trip. She was also perhaps the most courageous, and indomitable.

CHAPTER NINE

'Biafra'

To the public, missionaries exist for brief moments at times of violence, coups, famines and massacres. They perhaps remember Gladys Aylward and her heroic trudge across China with her little army of children singing 'Knick Knack Paddy Wack'. They remember a Holy Ghost Father telling of people buying a rat in 'Biafra' for £1, or Catholic nuns being raped and murdered in Congo, or Huddleston's stand against apartheid.

When violence explodes in a country, missionaries are often overtaken by circumstances. Oil men and other contract workers may feel that strife is not their business, and get out on the first plane. Missionaries tend to feel that they must stay. They identify with the people, and if they see those people going through hell they feel that to leave would be desertion. When we see missionaries at such moments, we see them at a testing time. Their normal stance of political neutrality may be in question. It may be almost impossible to do the right thing. They may even be blamed for having the courage to stay.

The Nigeria–'Biafra' war tarred many missionaries as 'pro-Biafran'; but the people we met would have helped the sick and the dying of either side. Many of them have not been allowed back to Nigeria.

During the last few days of the 'Biafran' collapse, we interviwed several missionaries as they came out. Many were too tired or shattered to talk. In this chapter we tell the story of one person who went through the agony.

*   *   *

Helen met Anne Bent one cold winter's day. She didn't look the part of the heroine.

H

I remember wondering how she had gone through it all, the throngs of hungry people, the terrible physical conditions, the dangers of the night flights to Uli. Here she was, dressed in a rather too long coat, with greying hair drawn from her face. She didn't look heroic or shell shocked: if anything just ordinary, quiet and shy. She wasn't a voluble talker and for perhaps the first hour I prodded her story out of her. It was amazing that this little woman who could so easily have been passed off in a crowd could have endured so much. She had displayed a greatness simply through her ability to be there and get on with her job. From what others have told us since we realize she was even tougher than we thought. I knew when I left, that she had been through something I could not have carried. She had a strength I did not have. I wanted to dismiss it—but I couldn't. Anne would have said there is a God who took her though this. Tritely I could say it was because she believed that she could endure. Sincerely, I can only say I don't know.

Anne's story begins in an ordinary enough way. She came from a good Anglican family in Wallasey and started nursing at seventeen, two days before the outbreak of the 1939 war. For many years she was a nominal Christian, but in 1949 she found in an Anglican nursing order and in CMS, two groups 'who didn't only run around talking. Commitment worked in their lives.' She offered herself as a missionary, and went to Iyenu Hospital in Nigeria, training midwives.

After fourteen months she came home on extended leave, feeling she had failed as a missionary even if not as a teacher.

Then in September 1955 Queen Elizabeth Hospital opened, and she went back to open the midwifery section. The hospital was a new and significant departure in mission policy: it was a United Mission project ,with many societies co-operating. They jointly put up the capital and the staff, and the short fall in operating costs was guaranteed by the government. It meant they could develop.

In 1965 she became matron, and enjoyed the job of building; the hospital was an experiment that worked. She remained matron through all the unrest and successive coups and crises.

The war was a surprise to her; along with many people she had regarded Nigeria as one of the more stable countries in Africa. She found it hard to accept the sudden Ibo zealotry and cliques

within the hospital; the sort of thing that led to 30 nurses volunteering for the militia on the outbreak of war.

With war came the first big exodus. All the companies recalled
their staff. She stayed. As her cook put it, 'You're not going,
you're mission.' She could see no reason for going and every
reason for staying. One sister told her 'with you people staying
it makes us still feel part of the world and we are not forsaken'.
Emotionally it was a difficult time because everyone who went
tried to persuade the others to go. 'It was a sort of phenomenon,
perhaps to bolster up their own position. "Let me know when
you're going and I'll come with you," they would say.' There
was such a panic they were ready to go without their possessions.
'It was much easier for oneself. My decision was made really
because there was no reason to go. Because you're a Christian,
you don't run away.' Then Nsukka fell and fighting approached
Enugu, capital of breakaway 'Biafra'. There was another exodus,
this time by boat. When Enugu fell, the nearby teaching hospital
evacuated and the Queen Elizabeth Hospital had to absorb 200
extra patients, three assistant matrons and an increase in doctors
to 30. They were by now geared to casualties, and knew time was
running out. 'The High Commission and its staff were leaving;
the hospital was now viable without us—should we get out?
We then decided each individual should decide. Nobody would
blame anybody. Three of us stayed, the bus manager, the medical
superintendent and I.'

Then food got short—for the staff too. May to August 1968
were terrible. She couldn't get through the patients in the wards,
they were so crowded. Pressures were so great that the missionaries who were staying were only doing six months stretches at
this stage; she came on leave for six weeks and returned to find
the whole hospital evacuated. All expatriate staff except missionaries had gone. 'We always said if the army collapsed and we had
no relief supplies we'd come out. We would only be an embarrassment then.' But she battled on and re-established the hospital
yet again in the shrinking enclave.

Anne said she felt an obvious sadness about the wasted years:
'One spent fifteen years building up something which is objecti-
vely wasted. But it did achieve something. There were a good
many trained midwives: one met our staff all over the country;
and they had established reputations.' Also, before war overtook

the situation, the experiment of the big Union mission hospital was already being copied elsewhere. The big mission hospital had been established as an answer to the problems of developing countries.

And Anne herself? 'I feel that this is the end of an era for me. Something else will open up that God wants me to do. It's too close to tell yet.' She felt very low immediately it was all over. 'I felt terrible over the week-end realizing how frightful it was for our people: the "Biafran" airport staff even thanked us for what we'd done which made it much worse. When you're working within the situation it's different. One of our doctors nearly killed himself with work: but when he came out he felt watching the tragedy on television was more emotional. For long periods we gave children inadequate amounts of milk knowing that it wouldn't stave off malnutrition, knowing they would come back. You've got to shut off things or you become unable to help. One has got to grit one's teeth and get on with it. We lived from hour to hour.'

It was terrible to come back to British affluence. 'Each time I come back this gets me. There are so many things people must have. First the television, then the fridge. And so it's gone on over the years. When one's gone back to essentials, you realize "things" don't make people happier. To me this is the crux of the Christian Gospel. I learned this through the war. All the rich people lost everything and were all reduced to the minimum.

'I don't think I switch back to this world very well. My last few leaves were spent in a bungalow on Loch Rannoch; an escape I suppose, but right away from the whirl of life. But I needed to get away from people and the telephone. It was a time for taking in and unwinding.'

One of the things the Nigerian experience had taught her was a different feeling about time. If you rush, she points out, you can save three minutes. 'What would I have done with the three minutes? I once had to wait two hours on Waterloo Station. I sat there and wondered where they were all rushing to. I was once a patient in QE with typhoid. Sometimes the nurses were very late and I was very impatient. But when they made the bed they did it as though I was the only person in the world. And for them I was.'

Months after we first interviewed Anne, and after she had

settled down to the routine of a job as senior midwifery tutor at
Newcastle-upon-Tyne Polytechnic, we asked her for her reflections on some of the extremes of contrast she had found coming
from a 'Biafra' situation to comfortable Britain.

In her work, she said, she found major differences. 'There seems
little sense of vocation among many staff here. People apply for
jobs not because they can give more, but purely for money.'
Anne was on the same allowance for sixteen years in Nigeria,
with nothing extra for her responsibilities as matron. She finds
the adjustment to a job rat race very hard to take.

In her personal life, she has lost an ability to enjoy food. 'One
of the joys of coming home on leave used to be to have a grilled
steak, rare, and salad and generally all those things one couldn't
get in Nigeria. But during my leaves from 'Biafra', and subsequently, I have really lost all caring for food. I like it well cooked
and tasty, but I'm not concerned as people in this country seem
to be to eat enormous quantities and spend a great deal of money.
Eating out really hasn't the same appeal it used to have. I'm not
trying to say this from any idealistic point of view. I don't look
at food and think of the starving children in Pakistan. There's
nothing of that sort. But during those three years I got into perspective what was important in life: primarily people; also how
little one needed to exist, to live and to live happily, as happily as
one can in any grim situation. You know as well as I do that
Britain and other Western countries are getting more affluent—
but not necessarily more contented.'

She enjoys, she says, some of the creature comforts that go with
the affluence—a rented TV set and a comfortable flat. She even
goes to the heights of luxury with a second-hand car purchased
for £80 which enables her to see friends and do missionary
deputation work. 'But in all the years in Africa we made our
own lives and enjoyed it without all the things people feel they
must have to obtain satisfaction in life.'

The hardest to take is the change in life style. 'In our hospital
compound in Nigeria, as probably anywhere in Africa, the doors
were wide open. People came and went, stayed the night, two
nights, three nights, three weeks, without anyone noticing their
coming. I used to go back for lunch and find my dining table set
for four and a guest installed in the guest room for a couple of
weeks. Back in this country we live in our flats with the doors

shut. People expect to be invited. They are most unhappy if one just calls—unless they happen to be overseas friends who are as delighted to have an unexpected guest as I am. We had friendships that developed quickly and lasted, both among our colleagues and among the nationals. It takes so much more time to develop here. There's a lack of *time* here. Everybody's rushing.'

One of the profoundest changes that came over Anne during the war period was that she became a pacifist. She had served throughout the 1939–45 war as a nurse. 'We all got completely swept up in the war effort and didn't have time—perhaps didn't even feel it right to think out—the Christian attitude to war; I certainly didn't.' Nor did she think much about it after the war. By the time the nuclear issue was sweeping Britain, she was out of the country. It wasn't until cessation between the Eastern States and the rest of Nigeria seemed inevitable that the issue had to be faced. 'I began to think with one or two of my colleagues about where we stood, and whether there was such a thing as a just war. In fact I took my stand on this before the war commenced and all the events of the following three years confirmed my belief that war should be avoided at all costs. The fact that schools and hospitals have to be rebuilt and re-equipped is a pity. But that isn't the tragedy. The tragedy is the loss of life, the bitterness created, the separation of families. We had one Ibo laboratory technician at Queen Elizabeth Hospital who was married to a girl from the River State. She is now in Port Harcourt with her daughter and he is in Umuahia with three sons. He can't go down to work in Port Harcourt, and because she's River State she's not acceptable back at QE. This is back to a state between the ethnic groups much worse than when we started QE.'

For some time, Anne thought of going back as a missionary. She has decided for the time being not to: it would be hard to find a place that could use her skills, and she didn't see her niche as a one-doctor bush hospital. Characteristically, she feels there is a tremendous challenge in this country. 'One feels the inertia and narrow mindedness of people, and the strong desire for security. I think one can bring to them a vision of other countries, and understanding of other nations. If all of us who are overseas remain overseas all the time there is no feedback. I think that just quietly living and working as I am doing here in Newcastle, with 400 staff and 4,000–5,000 students is important, particularly as people think missionaries are rather odd people. To find one on their staff is quite an eye-opener.'

To most people, 'Biafra' came and went as a nine-day wonder. It's just one of those things in the past. For Anne it will always remain more than that.

*   *   *

The Nigerian civil war faced the missionary leadership itself with redoubtable problems. Individual missionaries like Anne Bent carrying on a humanitarian job succouring dying people is one thing: their motives will be accepted even by those who dispute the wisdom of their actions. But when the Christian churches organize relief on the scale on which it was organized in the Nigerian civil war (50,000 tons of supplies transported by a specially purchased fleet of modern airliners, flying twenty and more flights a night) then relief itself becomes a political issue.

There were two major missionary societies involved in the Nigerian civil war, the Catholic Holy Ghost Fathers, and the Anglican Church Missionary Society; they were the societies who had the men on the ground, on both sides of the firing line, to administer the relief programme. The organization that supplied the planes and the food was a specially created European consortium of Catholics and Protestants called Joint Church Aid. The World Council of Churches was at one time involved, but withdrew when Nigeria refused to allow flights over her territory.

In the light of its experience of the Nigerian civil war, at least one of the bodies involved, the Church Missionary Society, has conducted a post mortem with a view to establishing guide lines for similar future conflicts. Mercifully, it has refused to duck the tricky political issues, or dress up its thinking in a load of verbiage and waffle.

'Let's face it,' the Rev. Canon John Taylor, General Secretary of CMS, said to his members at their annual general meeting in 1970, 'having discovered the surprising strength of innocence, we can never be innocent again. If co-operation puts aeroplanes into the hands of the churches they mustn't pretend the insouciance of St. Francis. Compassion on such a scale may be free from political or military motives, but it is certainly a political and military fact. If governments have been compelled to take seriously the possibilities of direct Christian action we must start to take them seriously ourselves.'

It may well be that it is impossible for the churches in a war situation to be a bridge to both sides. Given the emotions of war, the majority of people, Nigerian or European, Christian or humanist, reflect the same fear and hatred and anger as those around them. There are always the exceptions, and these are sometimes written up—retrospectively—as the saints. In the Nigerian war there were a few brave Nigerian Christians on both sides who argued steadfastly for reconciliation. They did this before hostilities actually broke out. They did it by meeting during the war on neutral ground in Accra and Lome; and they did it after the war by organizing messages of good will, gifts of money, foodstuff and salt. But they were, of course, the exceptions. And who are we, asks John Taylor, to find fault if they were few? 'There were not many Bishop Bells in our last European war.'

The world-wide Church was also on the horns of a dilemma. There were so many arguments for both sides, as there almost always are in a civil war situation. It was very arguable that fragmentation of Nigeria was the easy way out: if such a course were allowed, fragmentation would follow all over Africa, with disastrous economic consequences. But was it right to impose unity by starving millions into submission?

Again, once the war was on, did the relief effort merely prolong the war and indirectly destroy more lives than it saved? Nobody can be sure. It is arguable that had the Federal army overrun the Ibo heartlands a year earlier, before some of the most vindictive of the Federal commanders had been removed from the front, the behaviour of the troops and the ensuing panic might have led to far more terrible loss of life.

'There was never any clear Christian judgement leading the churches to declare that one outcome of the civil war must be right and the other wrong,' John Taylor says. 'Nor has victory itself in any way resolved the moral dilemma. It has merely, and mercifully, brought the killing to an end; it has not proved which side was right. . . Perhaps the moral perplexity suffered by so many Christians outside Nigeria who became emotionally involved in the struggle is part of the painful process of learning that a *simpliciste* view of right and wrong is always a fantasy which we ought to relinquish.'

CMS, as a society, steadfastly refused to take up a commitment for or against the 'Biafran' case, both because of these reasons, and because they had historical loyalties to all parts of Nigeria, and their missionaries were to be found on both sides of the conflict. But they did not interpret neutrality as withdrawal or passivity: like it or not, they were involved—'too much, no doubt, for clearsightedness', John Taylor admits. 'That was the extent of their identification with the people they had tried to make their own,' Taylor says. 'No Nigerian, no African, wants missionaries who are less identified, less committed. But let me repeat, they were not there to win a war for one side or the other. They were there, in the first place, because they were already on the spot when the war began: and Church leaders in Asia as well as Africa know that we have undertaken never to recall a missionary because of an emergency until they, the authorities of the local church, give the word that it would be better for the sake of the Church for them to go. The rest were asked to stay. To have withdrawn them at that point would have seemed a betrayal of friendship. And we have plenty of evidence that their costly and courageous staying put, on whichever side of the battle-line it may have been, was the most telling act of Christian witness that missionaries in Nigeria have ever been enabled to offer.'

Such a stance can be, and was, misinterpreted. It involved entry into a part of Nigeria without Federal permission; it involved defiance of the Federal authorities in flying in both missionaries and food. The Federal authorities claimed that this made nonsense of claims to neutrality. But neutrality does not mean pleasing both sides: this is impossible when one side does not even recognize the right of the other to exist.

Faced with all the perplexing claims and counter claims, the missionaries claimed that 'humanity comes first'. A Canadian journalist put it this way: 'The word was clear, without "ifs" and "buts". "Feed my lambs. Violate treaties, sovereignties and diplomatic niceties, be accused of taking sides, perhaps rule yourself out as a peace-maker—but feed my children."'

The lesson for the future, Taylor believes, is that the principle of sacrosanct national sovereignty has got to be challenged. 'I look forward to a day when all governments can take it for granted that wherever there is war or starvation or homelessness on any large scale, there the international Christian agencies of relief will quickly be at work in adequate strength serving the needy of both sides of any conflict, irrespective of the issues and, if negotiation fails, in defiance of sovereignties. I see this as part of the Christian realism which must protest that the little people in their particularity matter more than the structures which uphold and govern their lives.'

CHAPTER TEN

White Face, Black Africa

Missionaries don't have to go through revolutions or civil wars to face the political consequences of having a white face in the wrong place at the wrong time. Africa, Asia and Latin America are in ferment to throw off unnecessary culture from the West. And the missionary peddles an ideology as well as wearing a white face.

In some countries, such as Burma, this has meant the total exclusion of the missionary. In others, restrictive visa regulations squeeze the missionaries out one by one. In India all visas have to be renewed annually. Some countries, like Tanzania, have simply squeezed out the more fanatical.

Even where none of these explicit pressures exist, the pressures of working within a different culture remain. Imperialism may have gone, but economic imperialism is growing rather than diminishing; the sensitive missionaries fight to disentangle their ties with the West just as the more sensitive of the early missionaries fought to establish their independence of the traders and the imperial set-up.

*   *   *

In most developing countries the problem may never get as far as 'do as we say or you go' (although, as we shall see, that can happen). But the subtleties of cultural intercourse bug just about every missionary these days unless he's got the hide of a rhinoceros.

We commented to one East African that paradoxically there seemed to be more freedom of speech in South Africa than there was in his country. He said, 'Yes, that may be so. Freedom of speech is a luxury, and is everywhere relative. We can't afford it.

A handful of men with loudspeaker vans and leaflets could start a revolution here. We simply can't allow it.' If you utter platitudes about race relations, good will, or development, you will be fine. Question the credo of African socialism (in Tanzania) or Mercedes for the élite (in Uganda) or oathing (in Kenya) and you will be on a one-way ticket just as surely as any multi-racial troublemaker in South Africa. And for the more politically alert missionaries, who are desperately aware that all is *not* right with black Africa, this can be a galling situation.

One man told us: 'I attend conferences and seminars, and yet all the time one has to be holding back what one most passionately feels because one is a guest. No other frustration or difficulty bears the slightest comparison with the political sterility and lack of opportunity to voice or act on one's deepest convictions because of one's position as an invited expatriate missionary in a foreign country.' This particular missionary identified himself strongly with the poorest sections of his community, and knew only too well that a rich élite in Church as well as State was drifting inexorably further from the people. 'It disturbs me more than I can say,' he said, 'that we now have one theological college geared to producing clergy who are being adapted by their training-college life and heightened aspirations to an urban pastorate and the sophistications of urban living whilst the majority will be required to live under very simple conditions serving the peasant farmers who constitute the bulk of the population.' If the Church has any concern for social justice, he said, 'it will have to demonstrate that its own hierarchy does not belong to the élite at the expense of the common man . . . no episcopal palaces, church secretaries' large cars. . . One does just long to see some young clergy giving a lead as men who are on fire for Christ and as such are deeply committed to the cause of the "common man", are critical of gross social injustice and are prepared to preach—and suffer—at the hands of the élite the real implications of a society such as this. Instead of this the Church's newspaper is unwilling to print critical material, and when the editor did so, and was expelled, the hierarchy of the Church did not publicly back him.'

We came across a typical example of the kind of frustration that enforced silence or conformity can bring to the missionary in the story that a couple called the Ogdens told us about their time in the southern Sudan. The government suspected missionaries were buying popularity through their medical work, and ordered all missionaries to cease giving medical care. They found this very hard to take because Betty Ogden was a trained nurse. 'In the end we did give out medicines, illegally, and there were people sent out for this.' The tension they faced was whether they should come out into the open, knowing they'd be kicked out, or go on helping people quietly. 'I think we were right to carry on. Once we were all out we feared the worst for the people; the longer we stayed, even under the tensions, the better. One day a woman in an advanced state of pregnancy came in and Betty had to send her off to a government hospital; she overheard the people saying of her "She doesn't understand us". Betty was heartbroken.'

It was also heartbreaking in the last weeks to see RAF planes bombing the villages. 'The pilots said, "Well, we don't press the buttons". But it was the RAF chaps who serviced the planes. We just had to decide not to discuss politics and just try to live as normal a life as we could.'

Were they right? Genocide did break out in the southern Sudan once the Arab government to the north had squeezed out all missionaries. Was it right to stave this off as long as possible: or should they have made a short but brief outcry?

We found very few missionaries who would feel they had the right or duty to interfere. One missionary from Japan said: 'I'm not very good at speaking out and one feels as a guest that if one has political views one would keep quiet. Even if a minister was corrupt I don't think it would be my job to speak out.'

It is not in this realm of the prophet that most missionaries see themselves. Many are genuinely unpolitical, not because they identify with the establishment but simply because their canvas is a smaller, more personal one. Politics is just not their scene.

But no missionary can avoid the implications of indigenization. The missionary is now there, in virtually all cases, to work himself out of a job. Some missionaries see the withdrawal of Europeans as a matter of urgency; as long as the missionary is pulling the strings he is hindering rather than helping. This is why Huddleston left Africa, this is why a person like Laurie Campbell left his job as head of Alliance Boys' School in Nairobi: the very excellence of these men, their immense experience, was actually a barrier to African advancement. Huddleston's successor, Bishop Hilary, had none of Huddleston's flashing incisive drive and leadership. He was a gentle old man who got out his family photograph album and talked to us about his children and grand-children. He was a simple, pious and saintly man who was, we were told, a real 'father in God' to his people. Gone were the days when indigent priests could turn up at the Bishop's house and put in a soft touch for their needs, which would promptly be met from Huddleston's world-wide contacts. Masasi has slipped back into its backwater; parishes have *had* to stand on their own feet. As long as a European was there this couldn't happen. Huddleston wisely realized this.

Missionaries are reaping the fruit of a century of turning their backs on politics. Colin Morris, radical friend of Kenneth Kaunda, told us that one of his earliest memories as a young missionary in Northern Rhodesia was to attend his first staff meeting where the whole of a long and anxious meeting was devoted to a young African who had joined the African National Congress: could he stay or must he be fired? 'The politically conscious,' Morris said, 'were told by the Christian missionaries to zip up.' As a result, there was a leadership vacuum after independence. Men of spunk were anywhere but in the churches.

It is perhaps worth noting that where missionaries *were* out-spoken before independence, their courage earned them consider-able respect. One cabinet minister in Kenya told us that the real significance of Christianity emerged for him when it became apparent that missionaries fearlessly championed fair play during Mau Mau. 'People really noticed when missionaries sided with the underdog,' he said. Similarly, when Colin Morris shared a prison cell with Kenneth Kaunda under the white colonial administration, it is perhaps not surprising that he emerged as a personal friend and confidant of the President and, for many years, leader of the United Church of Zambia. Morris is very critical of many missionaries: 'The older brigade stuck with the colonial set up to the end,' he says, 'and gave the Africans as much of the Gospel as they wanted them to have.' The younger ones got involved in nationalist movements and saw them through to independence. 'Missionaries fulfilled their role on the boat back,' he said, and only those who spoke out before independence will be listened to today. 'If you kept your mouth shut you won't.

But anyway, the prophetic role is for the Church on the spot. These are the people who will go to the wall. The worst that will happen to the missionary (barring a Congo) is that he will be put on the first plane back. The task of missionaries who can speak out is to equip the Church on the spot to take up the prophetic role.'

The inexorable pressure for indigenization can lead to some heartbreak situations. One African recounted to us the story of a missionary who stood up at meeting, in tears, to ask if he was wanted any more. For fear of being regarded as a holy huddle of foreigners some missionaries have opted to cease meeting together as missionaries. Only in this way, they feel, can they demonstrate that they have sunk their aims totally in the local situation.

Sometimes the misunderstandings can be absurd. One missionary told us the story of the time he caused chaos in human relationships by apologizing. 'I was in a meeting, and was the only European. During the meeting I said something I later regretted and when I got an opportunity I apologized to the person concerned for being rather overbearing. He appeared to dismiss it and I felt the matter was settled. Later in the day, at a different session with different people, this man shouted with great passion "You don't know what it's like to be crushed". He wasn't addressing the remark to me, but I knew instinctively that he meant me; and after great reluctance he admitted it. To my astonishment he said that what had crushed him had been my apology. The reason, he told me, was that in his experience when a European apologizes it usually means he wants to gain the confidence of the African so that he can use that information against him. This hurt me. And it hurt me even more to discover that he seemed to be completely unaware that an expatriate could be hurt. He felt the only weaknesses I had were the weaknesses of strength; therefore it would be of little consequence to me that I had offended him—the only thing that would matter to me was academic interest of knowing what had offended him. When I said I was hurt that he could think me guilty of such things, it didn't seem to touch him.' We heard enough in similar vein to know that tortuous relationships worry a large number of missionaries.

Many of them would probably echo the feelings of the girl who related the story of one of her friends actually being sent home with 'culture shock'. 'I thought it rather amusing at first; but you can't fit in easily to a new society—for one thing the Africans do not accept you and they are just *not* black Europeans. I was rather disappointed to find the whites kept in a very closed huddle: I am still disappointed but I can understand it now.'

Criticism of missionaries amongst the leaders of new nations is sometimes harsh. 'Christianity ruled rather than served men in Uganda,' one African lecturer at Makerere said, 'It was haughty and superior... Christianity as a foreign import was pushed down people's throats and a little veneer of imperial rags obscured the fact that the religion was hollow, didn't have, because hadn't taken, any roots at all.'

'Christianity,' he said, 'could have learnt from the local context. Here was man, true man: not primitive. . . He had his ways, including religion: viable. He had a system or systems of belief and ethics. He had art forms: song and dance, poetry and drama, spoken literature. All these were labelled, when the question came up at all, as primitive, uneducated, sinful . . . and of course unchristian. Christianity refuses to confess that it is largely a shrine of European values and morals, and instead claims a universality which it patently doesn't have.

'As people wake up to these facts,' he said. 'They start their own breakaway, native, rebel churches.' These groups are growing in Africa. They now rival the major churches in numbers of converts and are a living reminder to present-day missionaries of the failure of their forebears. Todays' missionaries have the benefit of hindsight, and it makes them very cautious. They become almost neurotically introspective in their determination not to offend against today's culture; to the point where African colleagues are driven to frustration: 'They have become too sensitive for almost any kind of criticism.'

Some Europeans are very worried indeed about what they see as highly justified criticisms. Lutheran missionary, Rev. O. W. Nyblade, had this to say about cultural aggression: 'In our proclamation of the good news we are often guilty of cultural and personal aggression. Instead of having compassion on the multitude, we pity them because they do not have the "cultural advantages" that we have. . . Then when they react to our presence with hostility we take this as evidence not of our aggression against them, but of their "benighted nature," which justifies other acts of aggression on our part. . . In other words, it is difficult for us to accept people of other classes and cultures as they are, without trying to make them over in our own image. We fail to realize that this is a highly aggressive act. The good news of salvation in Christ brings meaningful and effective change in a society or culture only as it works within that culture. Too often we attempt to proclaim the good news through acts of cultural aggression. No wonder the fruit is sometimes bitter.

'A society, then, that is organized on highly competitive lines, in which some must be the losers and some the winners, should have a rather high degree of aggression and hostility manifested. The engine of competition, with its conflict, aggression and hostility, may result in some spectacular achievement. . . But on balance we must ask whether or not the losses in human values do not far outweigh the values gained in technological achievements.'

Another result of the fierce policies of indigenization is that Europeans are only able to operate at certain levels in the community. They can be top brain surgeons, engineers or academics. They can rarely assume positions of clerical leadership; the days of white bishops and headmasters are dwindling. Nor can they assume any position which exercises political leadership in Church or State.

Tom Houston, a leading Baptist clergyman we met in Nairobi, who has since returned to the UK, said to us, 'Missionaries must move with the times. And there are two times. You've got the old man still moving at the pace of three hundred years ago; and you've got the new who must be technical. The place for the Church is at the two extremes—in poverty and in the modern. We must leave the middle to the local. This is where the local people are competent. They are not at the frontiers of knowledge, nor, on the whole, are they altruistic enough to be at the bottom of the ladder. This is the challenge of leadership: unless you can work at both ends and in the middle you are negating the modern world. In this situation there should be as few missionaries as possible—in jobs without halos.'

To end this chapter, we want to instance the work of two people who seemed good examples of the new relationships that are essential in working as a modern missionary.

Sheilagh Warren was a teacher in the best girls' school in Uganda, which had been started by missionaries. She impressed

I

us with her tolerance and breadth of understanding. Some of the things she said to us in conversation indicate the very opposite of Western imperialist Christianity. Helen spoke to the sixth form and was surprised to find that the pupils did not even know that Sheilagh was a missionary. Sheilagh thinks this is a good thing. 'The word missionary is so totally misunderstood. I don't see why they should know we're missionaries. I should hope they would know we were Christians.'

Sheilagh Warren had a considerable respect for the culture and beliefs of the girls, and felt that she had no right to pressure them in any way to accept Christianity. 'You really cannot fire all your guns at minds that cannot compete with you on the same level,' she said. 'I think you have to open their minds, open doors for them to go through. I don't believe you should instill your deepest convictions into them. You can—but I don't believe you should.' She was convinced that there was a greater chance of people following a meaningful Christianity in this relaxed atmosphere; and anyway, she said, 'Education is not here to take the place of the past. It's here to build on it.'

The other person who showed most clearly the best of relationships between white and black, between foreigner and indigenous leader, was David Cowling, a Methodist agricultural worker whom we met at Meru in Northern Kenya. David was young, bearded, affable and quite unassuming. He would, he said, be just as happy working as a Christian in government as working for a missionary society. He worked perfectly easily under an African who was far less educated than he was, and yet was quite clearly the leader.

Lawi Imathiu, his boss, was president-elect of the Methodist Church of Kenya. Imathiu was in charge of 205 congregations and 10 ministers. Also young, he was straight and proud, with the bearing of a prince. He was a big, gentle man with an engaging smile. But when we met him, he was in no mood to co-operate. His opening remarks were brusque: 'So you think that British people are going to listen and try to understand us now just because you write this report, when for two hundred years they haven't listened?' He proceeded to grill us on whether we really saw that the missionary thing was *totally* different than anything pre-independence. But having established our bona fides, in answering a number of blunt questions, Lawi softened, and we began to see the qualities that marked him out for leadership. He was, he said, more than happy to see missionaries—of the right kind—continuing to come to Kenya. His country was short of technicians, doctors and specialists of all kinds, and would be for a long time. He felt it would be a tragedy if the government should ever stop missionaries from coming. 'Without ideas coming in from outside you are so limited. I cannot see a time when there will be no missionaries. There is no church that can stand alone without missionaries.'

He described missionaries perhaps as well as anyone we met. 'I would say missionaries are not a special people. But they have an ideal of service. They have compassion to human needs. And they are willing to work under difficulty in conditions an ordinary Englishman would not accept.'

Imathiu had no illusions about ordinary Englishmen. He had been to England to study, and whilst he was there propounded views of his own about the need for two-way missionaries, only to be directed to the blacks. 'There are a lot of your people in Wolverhampton and the Midlands. Why don't you go and bring *them* back to the Church?' When he did hospital and prison visiting, he said, 'people would accept you with their lips. The answers you got were Yes, No, Yes, No—and that means you go.' He knew only too well the studied politeness that can be as warm and welcoming as a wet fish. And now, back in Kenya, he was determined that those working within the Church should be totally accepting—both ways. 'You come,' Lawi said, 'And we accept you up to a point. But after that we begin to ask if you will fit in or not. Very few Africans accept easily.'

The relationship between Imathiu and Cowling was striking. On the one hand Lawi, who has only primary school education, has a natural leadership. It is he who naturally takes up the key issues. It was he who risked his neck in protesting to the government about the reintroduction of oathing amongst the Kikuyu. 'If there is injustice in my district I do not wait for the churches to speak out. I go straight to the top. . . The Church must be a prophetic Church or it is nothing.'

David, degree and all, was content to serve. 'There have been three eras of missionaries in Kenya,' he said. 'The first were pioneers and dictators, the second paternalists, and the third are here to serve.' He may have had the specialist knowledge to supervise a couple of agricultural extension farms, a mobile education service and a major settlement project, but he found it completely natural to work under the maturity of Imathiu's leadership. 'We came to an autonomous church and people of our age take it easily.'

David told us that many of the older men simply can't do this. They find it hard to see what the younger men take for granted— the fact that technical knowledge and experience in themselves are less important than simple relations. 'Many of them quietly accepted this, and have gone,' David said. As a couple, he and his energetic little wife, Megan, are very informal and fit in naturally with the local people. For them, the opportunity to stand outside Western civilization had been good. Many, many people whom we spoke to on the trip made the same point. They all valued the sense of timelessness. In the West, David said, 'timekeeping and efficiency are becoming more important than personal relations. Africa puts the individual back into perspective.'

CHAPTER ELEVEN

'Wholesome and Godly Examples'

The trip through Africa was a kaleidoscope of impressions of languages, tribes, colourful costumes and good works. We kept trying to focus on 'the missionary'; but it was not until two o'clock one morning arguing with two 'missionary couples', that it suddenly dawned on us that these were people, just plain ordinary accountants and journalists. To be sure, they had decided to work for God, and this marked them out strongly in the matter of their beliefs. By that decision, by that label 'missionary', they were categorized; and like diehards talking about 'youth', we were trying to put these two couples on a cheese board and label them 'missionary'.

We're not saying that being religious, and being religious in a job overseas, doesn't put them a world away from ordinary folks; but their stomach-aches feel just like ours. And in the same way they are subject to jealousy, anger, family problems and naughty children.

There were as many missionary types as there were people we met. There were tight up judging ones; there were jolly roly-poly ones; there were shy little old ladies; there was unsquashable Stephen Carr. All were missionaries, some accepting and liberal, some as hard boiled and fundamentalist as they come.

Again, many missionaries have families. And the wives, for all their husbands may be doing, are often ordinary English women you could meet on a housing estate. They work in all kinds of different countries trying to stand up for what their husbands are doing. Some had delightful modern houses and acres of lawn, with servants, books, all mod cons. Others were landed with creaky dark old missionary relics for homes.

In this chapter we have tried to show some of the personal and family problems. They vary according to remoteness, country, and climate. Most of the families we met were cheerful about the problems they faced, and this contrasted strongly with many of the families of other aid workers we met.

From the day when they receive 'the call', missionaries face many pressures. They accept a way of life that is vastly different; they live in one continent and have their families and home in another; they may face isolation. (One family we met had been living 200 miles from the nearest other English family.) They face Africanization, political upheaval, or parental opposition; they endure the shock of commuting between affluence and poverty; and through all this they have to try to live up to ideals which only saints attain.

From the start, they are dogged by their image. Much more than 'school-teachers', 'school workers', 'politicians' and other groups of people we put in little boxes, 'missionaries' are lumped together into a single, monolithic and foreboding stereotype. The fact that this stereotype bears little resemblence to the reality does not affect the fact that it is the image, and it has been lived up to. It is the first of the pressures.

Many of the newer missionaries find this hard to take. When we arranged a meeting of 'missionary wives' at Selly Oak Training Colleges, Birmingham, one wife said the classification as a 'missionary wife' made her feel as though she was in a zoo being looked at. A girl who was a hostel warden at an African university said that if she was labelled 'missionary' her relationship with her students would be hopelessly damaged. Missionaries we talked to from Libya, Iran and other Muslim countries begged us not to tag them with the label: it could lead to expulsion. Another girl said that her childhood memories of missionaries from her father's days in the Colonial Service were hardly flattering: 'From what I'd seen they lived a dreadful life. It seemed so hard. Most of the ones I'd met had been rather dried up spinsters.'

There are two aspects to the image that the younger missionaries don't like: firstly that they are set apart as 'good'; secondly that missionaries are people that 'get at you'. One young doctor told us that he could hardly communicate with his father over his decision to become a missionary; the only comment his father had made was to blurt out on one occasion 'For goodness sake don't get a Jesus complex when you go to Africa, or anything like that.'

'In other words,' the doctor said, 'he could only see anyone going for their own glory, they were trying to become great Albert Schweitzers. He couldn't see that anyone might not consider themselves an Albert Schweitzer or a Jesus Christ or anything else, that he might just be a bloke, with a sort of ideal.' His father was not exactly a keen Christian. 'I don't think he'd call himself anything at all. I think he'd say "this is a Christian country" sort of thing and he's part of it.' This same doctor felt that his friends 'impose the Jesus Christ complex on you. They think you are doing something very exceptional by being a missionary doctor, which to them still has the aura of something rather magnificent. You really must be rather wonderful people. We're not at all. We're very ordinary people in the same way they are. It's difficult coping sometimes. People think you're pious even if you're not. And I don't think I'm pious. I don't think I'm any better than anybody else. This is the whole point of Christianity.'

Whatever may have been the inner voice of the people we met, few of them seemed to think themselves holier than the rest of us. Being 'good' was simply something they had to live down. When we said to one group of missionary wives in Uganda that 'being good' was one of the principal attributes of the missionary wife, there were hoots of laughter. But whether they like it or not, the missionary and his wife inherit haloes as surely as kings inherit crowns. And this can be hard on some wives, who may have fallen in love with a guy who was an accountant, teacher or medical student, only to find him turn out a missionary. They join him, because their heart leaves them no choice. Henceforth they will be judged as he is judged. When visiting writers, like us, pitch up they will dutifully bring out the tea, wear a skirt of modest length and keep the children quiet. They must, as the Ordering of Deacons puts it, be 'wholesome and godly examples and patterns for the people to follow'. The pressures to be the perfect wife, the shop window for Christian family life, can be absolutely killing. You are just as much a prey to anger, fluctuating emotions and period tensions as anyone else. And yet the myth dictates that you do not show it. You smother your emotions with results far more cloying and dishonest than outright anger.

Funnily enough, we, too, found ourselves contributing to the stereotype. We were shocked at swear words where we would never have noticed them in 'normal' company; we noticed in detail the faults of wives who seemed less than perfect or less than loving. The wives themselves contributed to it: after getting to know us one girl laughed and admitted that the cake was baked only because some writers were coming: 'I thought I ought to do this: I always do. It's the kind of thing that's expected of a missionary's wife.'

An American wife summed all this up with her simple plea: 'I wish people would see me as normal. Sometimes I feel like saying "Gee, I don't know why your Uncle Al died any more than you do!"'

*   *   *

Families usually get a furnished house and there are residential centres for them back in the UK. They go out on 'tours' of, usually, four years. In the old days most went 'for life'. Today most recruits don't plan to stay beyond their first one or two tours. This impermanence may make the adjustments more difficult.

Some people coped with terribly primitive conditions, teaching their own children, enduring blistering heat (maybe all combined) with great cheerfulness. Others seemed to baulk at just about everything. We felt they'd be happier back in England—and probably they do go back as soon as the first big hurdle comes along.

Anne Carr was the supreme example of taking all the hurdles without one look back: isolation, danger, hard work, sometimes primitive conditions, educational problems, three changes in language, sudden moves, a very occupied husband. But this is a way of life that she doesn't question.

Other young wives see learning a new language as a major problem. If they changed after two years as Anne had done they would feel it as a real set back. Not many people would have camped in game country in a tent, with an adopted baby, and built their own mud and wattle hut. Most would feel that a fridge and cooker were essential; certainly one Oxfam wife we spoke to thought that their £500 furniture allowance was incredibly small. Anne and Stephen built their *home* for £140.

Isolation not only means difficult physical conditions, it also means that the missionary couple become message carriers, shoppers, ambulance drivers and source of news and knowledge and advice for the local community. Most wives run a dispensary. This means that an incredible amount of extra work is put on them.

A marriage will be under terrific strain, and isolated communities often have a lot of in-fighting. Hospitals especially have great flare-ups.

Probably the biggest pressure missionaries have to face is education for their children. When we first looked at the subject we were inclined to think in simplistic terms: if the missionaries love and serve the people they go to work amongst, surely they would send their children along to the local schools, they would identify totally with the local people. After all, in the main they are not living amongst primitive peoples. The new nations have an infrastructure of good schools, even if they are only few in number. This view was put to us very strongly by a number of African critics. Even high clerics seemed hurt that almost to a man the white missionaries in their midst either packed up and went home when their children reached secondary school age, or sent their children back to English boarding schools. 'If they regard the schools they run as good enough for our children why aren't they good enough for theirs?'

The reality, as we came to understand, is different. Even before school age there are problems. It is difficult to transport all the toys, books and play equipment an English family would take for granted. The parents therefore have to make a special effort during the formative play years to see a child is not under-stimulated. When African children come to play they may regard the little white child with his comparatively huge amount of toys as the leader and this creates an unhealthy bossiness in the white child.

Then, there are no comparative primary schools. Africans usually start school at seven or eight with no reading or background or previous experience of books and toys. Instruction is in a foreign language. If you want your child to go back into the English educational system, you have to give private help. Usually the mother takes on the whole job of teaching the children to read, write and grasp the basics of primary education, often using the Parent National Education Union designed for overseas parents. Some parents find the job of teaching easy, but Niall and Sheila Watson in Kenya had a bad situation with their seven-year-old. He had to be driven 25 miles twice a day to school on a very bad road. This was cutting into Niall's work time, but they felt he would never see children his own age if he stayed at home; and Sheila had enough on her hands with two smaller children, a dispensary and all the other calls on the wife of a missionary who becomes social worker, counsellor, and source of loans for the whole community.

The only other choice is boarding school, which most mothers put off as long as possible. 'I taught him for two years, then when he was seven we hummed and ha'd and broke our hearts and sent him away to boarding school because he was beginning to resent my teaching him. A lot of mothers can't cope, and send their children to boarding school at the age of five. I couldn't bear it; that's why I didn't do it.'

With secondary schooling the critical educational problems arise. The crunch issue is that educational certificates issued in Africa or Asia would not be recognized as entry qualifications for British universities. Then there is the cultural issue: is it right that children should grow up with the attitudes of one culture only to be forced to adapt to another on the almost inevitable return of their parents to the United Kingdom?

In India and Japan there are English language secondary schools, and although this almost certainly means boarding, at least the children are nearer. Where missionaries had permanently identified themselves with a country—even this had not entirely solved the problem. One missionary family have served in Ruanda and Uganda since 1923, and have now retired to end their days in Kampala. One of their sons, born in Uganda, felt very much out of things in England, being regarded as a colonial at best, a foreigner at worst. All his roots were in Uganda, and now after qualifying as a doctor, he has gone back. But he is very definitely a man strung between cultures. Although he loves Uganda, he is not regarded as Ugandan by the Ugandans; and England is in no sense his home.

What it really boils down to is that missionaries are prepared to make sacrifices themselves but not to handicap their children. No one can guarantee them a future in Africa or Asia, so they plan for a return to the United Kingdom.

There are a lot of minor problems relating to insecurity and discipline and crossing cultures. 'In Africa the children may piddle indiscriminately in the great outdoors; they wouldn't do this back here!' Or again, 'We want the children to have right attitudes rather than be "good". But the Japanesse children are terribly good, clean and docile. It looked pretty awful if our children were too rampagious.' Children suffer their own particular problems coming back to the UK. They have to spend much more time indoors. 'One dreads leave slightly because of the children living in other people's houses in case they spill things on the carpet. In Africa we have concrete floors and sisal mats. Children bring a bucket of sand into the living room and empty it and no one turns a hair. Then there is the problem of noise. It's deafening here in England. In Africa you have all the windows open.'

Some families have a long and happy tradition of missionary service over several generations; the most striking example of this was the Church family, in which over 100 members of the family have been missionaries since the eighteenth century. Four of the eight children of the Teichlers (Chapter 8) have followed their parents into missionary service, and we met at least a couple of dozen other cases in which a close relative had been a missionary. Several told us of the impact that some early missionaries had had on their minds, ranging from romantic ideals of service to simple admiration and respect for the qualities of the men and women.

In other cases, being brought up in a missionary household produces a diametrically opposite effect. We knew of two young hippies who rejected their parents' faith, and some of the children told us of the claustrophobic effect of spending a fair amount of their childhood in the company of elderly spinsters and earnest gatherings of visitors. 'Going to an ordinary British school and hearing swear words and seeing the absence of my parents' values was a great shock. It made me question everything.' Even if there were aspects of the missionary life against which they rebelled as children, the ones we met all profoundly respected their parents. One young chap at university, for instance, simply could not bring himself to admit to his father that he was an agnostic, because he respected him and his work so much that he didn't want to hurt him.

In the end, the overall educational experience can be a blessing. As one missionary from Japan put it, 'the children benefit enormously from learning that there is a huge culture that is not British'. One mother who'd been in India told us that her boy had come top of general knowledge. 'We had an enormous library,' his mother said, 'because we've always believed in books. We sold 300 children's books before we came back and we must have bought twice as many as that, mostly Ladybird and paperbacks. I think the education experience was a positive one. It seems to me that my children had a much wider experience of life. You never knew quite who you were going to meet. You mix with Americans, Australians, Canadians, people from all over the world. Our youngest goes to school and says she has seen elephants. "On the telly?" "No, no this was *real*." '

*   *   *

Another strain is the worry about their parents and families back home. In part this is simply being on the other side of the world, and a long way from ageing and possibly sick parents. This is often a reason for finally deciding to pack it in. A more serious strain arises when there is subdued or active hostility from the parents to the whole business of being a missionary. At its worst, this can lead to a case we came across where wealthy parents had disowned their daughter when she married a missionary; they did not relent even when she had children—when she came back to the UK with her husband, she received a message 'Please do not contact us'. Even when she was seriously ill and near death, the cable sent to inform her parents was ignored. Although this is an extreme case, we found many couples who had suffered some degree of estrangement from their family and friends. 'They think it's wrong to take three young children,' one doctor's wife told us. Her husband had left the RAF to become a missionary, and her parents see the children taking all sorts of risks. They are against the whole idea of going: there is plenty of need here, they say, without going to Africa. 'When it really comes to it you say God is calling you, and you are up against a brick wall. They just don't understand. They can't understand us giving up the security—my husband would have been a Group Captain by now. But they are in their sixties, and it is almost certain one of them will die while we are away and they can't look forward to this.'

Another girl said: 'When I got involved with the Church that was the last word. My father was angry and bewildered. When I went further and married a clergyman he just felt it put us apart from him. I'm fond of my father but we're different now. Both my parents are in their seventies and I feel certain they won't be there when I get back. Part of the problem is that our parents know "missionaries" and they know all our faults and we just don't fit into their idea of missionaries.'

Again, another young doctor: 'It's very frustrating for us. There is a total lack of communication between us and my parents. There's just no way of getting it across. They're nice kind people, but there's no starting-point for discussion. When discussions do come they tend to be awfully short one-word answers to aggressive questions from my father. There's a total breakdown of communication, that's what it boils down to. I can't think of any other way of expressing it.'

*　　*　　*

What do all the pressures of missionary life do to the marriage relationship? In many ways this was one of the most difficult questions to fathom. Missionaries in general are not very forthcoming about sex, and you can hardly go round as a two-day guest asking 'How good is your marriage?' Statistics of divorce don't help because missionaries don't believe in divorce and will soldier on with grim determination, loyalty or stubbornness. But some very definite points did emerge in talking to scores of missionary couples.

Much more than in suburban Britain, man and wife are thrown together. They not only spend their sleeping and leisure hours together, they frequently work together. In many cases they are also completely isolated, which throws them still further upon each other. This increases the stresses if things go wrong, but it can strengthen the marriage. There is no mental divorce, with the wife knowing nothing of the husband's work.

The wife may not have the specialist skills of her husband, but she will frequently share or support his work. The relationship can deepen and develop in a way that is impossible when a man has a nine-to-five job. You can seldom ask a woman complicated questions about her husband's job and get such detailed and perceptive replies as we had from wives like Angela Mockford. They were truly working colleagues and had a role which was totally equal and important. Purely from an outsider's vantage-point it seemed that some of their marriages were the closest we'd ever seen.

At one stage, the role of wives in the missionary situation was very much undervalued. Until 1951, unless they were specialists in their own right, their sole claim to fame in one missionary yearbook was the letter 'm' for married, tacked after their husband's entry. Few missionary societies would make this under-valuation today, and the wife is listed as a missionary in her own right.

All this said and done, some people seemed to have dried up and sterile relationships. In one case a most brilliant and able doctor was married to a wife who was a total and unmitigating nagger. Everywhere we went we saw the respect the staff had for him, the creativity he put into his work, his drive. All we heard from her about him was critical, undermining and denigra-tory. But his reaction was one of complete patience. He was as gentle and accepting as she was carping.

In another case it was as clear as daylight that the wife had no real empathy for the husband's work. Every reason was advanced why they could not continue. Everything was wrong and we felt she might force him to give up his work. Since our visit they have pulled back from the frontier situation he was pioneering.

The husbands weren't all angels either. Especially where the work was 'all-important' and the man (to us) more fanatical, the wife was often subjugated. Once or twice men actually did a double take when we said we wanted to interview their wives. Somehow, anything that wasn't 'the work' was not important. We felt that in a number of cases women were doing a much more difficult job than their husbands in coping with several children and awkward conditions, the climate and the missionary work. Yet their contribution was completely ignored.

But these were exceptions. In most cases, we suspect, we did not see the failures.

*   *   *

Poverty is quite a different problem. Missionaries, according to the image, are supposed to be poor. And to a degree they are. They don't always find it easy to accept the relative poverty; 'the poor paupers of the managing directors up the hill and the rich uncles of the Africans down below', as John Mockford put it. It is particularly hard when they see the affluence of Britain. But money is surprisingly absent from missionary conversation. We must have stayed with or talked to nearly 200 missionaries, without one of them beefing about money. And as this is, apparently, the major cause for discord amongst married couples in the UK, ranking even higher than sex, it is significant.

There is, a quite conscious attempt to give up the material things of this world, even amongst the newer missionaries. New recruits told us of their unease as all their friends bought fitted carpets and slipped into middle-class living. They were often glad to be released from the rat race.

But with furnished homes supplied, access to cheap transport, free passages and medical aid, help with education and a low cost of living, the missionaries we met were not 'poor'. As one missionary society put it: 'We have 170 years' experience of this business; it is short-sighted policy to cripple a man with money worries. He should be free to do his job.'

Missionaries also seem to feel a real bond of loyalty to their sending society. They know that anything they save will go on furthering the work. A few years back, at a time of financial difficulty, the headquarters staff at BMMF, from the General Secretary to the office boy, voluntarily accepted a 5% reduction in salaries to avoid cutting back on the overseas work; and this in a year when prices rose 10%. Again, missionaries who accept government positions often opt to have their salaries paid direct to the sending organization; they go on drawing their old allowances. There is no contractual, moral or legal compulsion to do this; it is just indicative of an attitude to money and to service. Certainly there is a marked difference in the attitude of missionaries compared to many workers in British charities. There is often a great deal of bitterness about salaries in charities. And where sacrifices have been made, there is sometimes little modesty in saying so. An individual may feel he is happy to accept a reduction in salary because he believes in the cause. He is not likely to remain so happy if he finds that others in the same organization have not taken such a drop. There is also perhaps less of a binding force between individual workers, who may be thrown together by the cause, but no common philosophy.

Missionaries, essentially, are unworldly people. Perhaps if they do have resentments, it is that having decided to accept a big drop in potential and actual earnings, the public still won't leave them alone. It's almost as though the public has a vested interest in their conscience. 'The last time I was home,' one of the wives told us. 'I bought a white coat and I thought it was actually very attractive. But I was told "How do you expect people to give money if they see you so well dressed?"' Even frankness doesn't always help. Wendy Williams of Uganda told a meeting back home that she actually had a higher standard of living in Uganda than she had had in Bromley. She described her delightful bungalow, surrounded by lawns and flowering shrubs, and explained she had good furniture, kitchen equipment and servants; but nobody believed her. 'Go on, Wendy,' she was told. 'We all know what you suffer and go through.'

*   *   *

Servants are another problem. Some missionaries take to them like a duck to water: 'I've no feeling of compromise about this. People employ people in England; if my car goes wrong I take it to someone—I respect him for being able to do it. In a rural situation it's a full-time job keeping alive. You have no running water, no electricity. I can't see any question of principle involved. A foreigner who did not employ servants would be considered most undesirable because he is depriving an Ethiopian of employment.' But by no means all missionaries feel like this. Having people to wash your underclothes and wait at table and change the babies' nappies inevitably means that you slip into a life, if not of ease, at least of acceptance of the rich-poor divisions. However much you justify this by rationalizations—labour is so cheap, it helps to employ people, time is at a premium—some missionaries have their nagging doubts.

We personally found it strange to arrive at a missionary guest house to see white-robed servants padding around like unobtrusive shadows. They seemed not merely servants but servile. When we queried this it was pointed out that this was the accepted role of servants in any relatively wealthy African household; servants were, we were told, treated far worse in many private households. But this was hardly the point. Missionaries had no compunction about changing the habits they didn't like. There could at least be introductions. This never happened to us in missionary households. Ever.

This is not to be moralistic: but it is a difficulty for the more sensitive missionaries. On the whole, some form of household assistance is obviously essential for missionaries. Some of them face mountainous problems of hospitality. One woman we spoke to in Uganda had had 132 overnight visitors the previous year. But the basic problem of relating to a servant class seems to remain, and some missionaries told us that although they had no problems relating to the educated, were they saddled with an irrational sense of guilt as they tried to pick their way through the tortuous problem of servant relationships.

* * *

Perhaps the biggest heartbreak is finally saying goodbye to missionary work. In all probability you will be hastening the day when someone else fills your job and you have to leave. And if you have fallen in love with a country like India or Kenya this comes very hard.

Even returning to the UK between four or five-year tours is not easy. To those who regard England as 'home' there is often deep shock at the affluence and greed they find upon their return: 'On leave this last time I had one very poignant moment. I was waiting for a bus and it just struck me—here were all these people flooding out with great piles of groceries. So much money was pouring over the counter without anyone even noticing it at all. And we had been told how poor everyone was meant to be and how desperate Britain's economy was.' Again in similar vein: 'You are freer to leave the rat race alone when you are abroad. Taking the children to school here and just standing around is a shock. The talk is all of the second car. It just made us laugh at talk of "Britain's economic crisis".' A missionary who had worked in the Bihar famine said that the British Rail catering poster just floored him: 'Don't just stand there—eat something.'

K

Another Indian missionary felt the same: 'It's the shock of coming out of this need. There's obvious need, and you arrive back in this country and everybody seems so self-satisfied and complacent, jogging along in their own clean tidy comfortable ruts. Nobody wants to know about India, or very few people. My relatives, I mean they're all really quite close to us, sending us magazines and things, but they haven't asked us a single question about the work. It's a bit of a shock when you've been away for four years and you're still really in another place.'

A lot of missionaries don't like the changes they find: 'During our absence everything seems to have increased. Sexy advertisements have become more so. Expensive things are up still further. The minimum level of existence seems to go up and up. Colour television is now a necessity.'

They also find it hard to re-adapt to the famed reserve of the English. 'You don't feel you can just drop in on people as you do in India, because in India all the British people seem to hang together and you can call in on anybody whether you know them very well or not. It doesn't seem to matter how many of you there are, they'll fit you in.'

Some of them on their return simply find it hard to cope with the ordinary things: 'On leave from Nigeria I had very little idea how to organize myself. I was in a flat with no help, no garden, no washing machine and four of my six young children under five. I hadn't done any cooking or housework for four years. The sheer mechanics of having to cope with all these small children, added to my haemoglobin count of sixty was almost too much for me. I went most peculiar. I just had to struggle and struggle and struggle to keep going at all. Sometimes I just gave up and went to pot because I was too tired to cope. I couldn't manage the housework or bedmaking or washing or any of the things competent mothers are supposed to do. I just stopped doing it. I hadn't the energy, I hadn't the will. Then you'd go out and see all these other people coping splendidly and you'd feel even worse.' This mother told us that she actually reached the point at one stage, of nearly throwing the baby across the room. At that stage she realized how far things had gone, and 'phoned her husband in desperation: this sort of incident perhaps helps to emphasize the humanity of missionaries.

Perhaps most difficult of all to take is ignorance of, and apathy towards the work they are doing. This is partly caused by the rich–poor gap. One missionary from Ethiopia said 'What can I tell people? There is nothing like Ethiopia in the UK—fifty years ago this wasn't true. You could point to something say "It's like that". Three hundred years ago it was probably identical.' Another from Africa said: 'We were struck by the terrible ignorance about Africa, even with TV. Around my area of East Anglia you show slides and get comments like, "Oh! Don't they look clean"—and this from an educated man—or "Some of those faces look really intelligent". You show a picture of your house and you get a few gasps which show what they thought you were living in. Slides help to remove this—but they're not much help in the deeper problems.'

A missionary from Iran told us: 'When I talk about modern cities the questions really suggest everyone lives in mud huts and has loin cloths. I tell them that our buses—made in Iran—have toilets at the back, reclining seats and TV over the driver's head.'

*   *   *

One wife of a missionary doctor in Botswana more or less sums up the kind of pressures we have talked about and shows what happens when several problems are compounded. The couple concerned were South Africans, serving in a multi-racial country. The border between the two countries was a couple of hundred yards away: you could see the lights of the South African border post as we sat out in the evening. Just the other side of the border, in very desolated country, was one of the areas chosen by the South African authorities for their 'dumping grounds' for endorsed-out people. These endorsed-out people were of the same tribe as the local Botswana people, and feelings were running high. At the same time the doctor and his wife were often rejected by their friends in South Africa; certainly going to serve Africans is not 'normal' to Afrikaan South Africans.

Mrs. Schmidt was a charming woman, struggling to help her husband run a big hospital, coping with several children, living in an attractive house with lawns, flowers and modern furniture.

'The younger missionaries coming out here are finding it more and more difficult. They do have strong ties back home in Europe and so they always have this escape. But so many people just can't adjust. My husband says many people develop actual physical symptoms which are just a result of the work. He has just examined one such person from the Republic who developed terrible backache. My husband knew there was no physical cause. They just feel "What am I doing here?" and they can't go on. All of them at the hospital are so overworked. Many are managing jobs they aren't trained to do and we wives watch our husbands overworked and unable to reach through.

'I feel the strain every summer. The heat is terrific. We close the windows and draw the curtains every day to try to keep the cool air in. I have aged so much in five years. I have days when I could weep I'm so exhausted. I feel I can't give the support to my husband I should.

'There's no real social life here. A lot try to make friends among the Botswana. One person we knew did have real friends, not just acquaintances. But he is an artist and I don't feel he has his feet on the ground.' The isolation has big effects. 'Being cut off from your relatives is terribly hard; for instance, if you go into confinement you are completely alone and have no relatives or friends.

'There is a strain when the children go away and when they come back the primitive way of life affects them. The houses here are so poor. And the better your house is, the more guilty you feel. Yet we must also keep up a standard for our children. They don't want to come back if you are too primitive. Often I wonder whether our big white house isn't an obstacle in contacting the people. It's a peculiar thing because if heart speaks to heart it can be understood through any barrier; but then you've got to be very open.

'One of the biggest strains in the missionary life is being with other missionaries; sisters, for instance, who have to both live and work together. Their personalities are grouped together through no choice of their own and their stresses have repercussions on the whole small community. This trouble is always there and takes different forms. I couldn't stomach this at first; why, in a missionary set-up, there should be so much fighting. And when people care too much they fight even more. Usually the issues that cause the final flare up are not big—like somebody being late for supper. I suppose it's something like "expedition neurosis". People are grouped together without letting off steam.

We need something like cracking cups or something to let off steam. Missionaries in particular feel more guilty if they get cross. They want to be an example to people around them; but if they succeed in controlling tempers they sometimes become too controlled.

'You do have a picture of what people should be like. I came to a point at one time when I said: if Christians are like this, I don't want to be a Christian.

'Even the African nursing staff are nervous in our house. You can see it the way they hold their cups. We have a more relaxed social meeting if we play games on the lawn. People here do try to overcome these barriers. The Africans get very pally, but we feel there is no heart to heart contact. It's almost like a squire's house in England. The European is probably most to blame because we don't face it. My husband and I feel that there is no one we could say is a friend. We feel very very lonely.

'These five years have been tremendously important from a religious standpoint. We have deepened our understanding of the message of Christ. You have no distractions here. You have to face yourself. You can't run away from it or go to the cinema. Every time you preach something you have to look at yourself. You even say prayers with a group who see you twelve hours every day. And in the end you don't want to run away.'

CHAPTER TWELVE

The Oxfam Temptation

The scale of world-wide missionary endeavour is probably much bigger than most people imagine. It is hard to get comprehensive figures because the work is fragmented amongst several hundred Catholic and Protestant organizations. But some idea can be gained just by glancing at some of the statistics.

The *World Christian Handbook of 1968*[1] reported over 31,000 Protestants ordained and lay missionaries at work in 1968. There were 54,000 Catholics, including over 14,000 missionary priests in Africa and Asia. Ireland alone sends 7,085 priests, nuns, brothers and laity from 95 different orders. England and Wales (long considered by Catholics as a mission field itself) sends another 1,625.

With something like 85,000 expatriate missionaries scattered over the globe, plus an even larger number of indigenous priests and church workers (Indian Catholics priests now outnumber non-Indian by over three to one), the churches represent one of the biggest development forces in the world. Two Church agencies alone (Church World Service and Caritas) have budgets over the $100 million mark. Of the $900 million a year that is reckoned to be the total of private, non-governmental aid to developing countries, more than half goes through Church outlets.

Perhaps more important than the quantity of aid is the quality. And it is quality that missionaries justifiably stress. The people of the developing world are not going to thank the West if all we have done through 'development' is to encourage the kind of greed *we* have. The West may destroy the good in primitive and tribal societies and replace it with a rapacious capitalism, even

---

[1] *World Christian Handbook* (1968), Lutterwoth Press.

if this passes as 'development' in economic terms. This is where missionaries, who hold steadfastly to values other than materialism, may score. Many missionary projects are perenially short of money, and people become jacks of all trades, and this is good in a primitive society where 'experts' aren't needed as much as good all-rounders. Missionaries also stay longer than secular aid workers. The Catholics especially and many Protestants, are unattached and can give everything to their work. And they work for love, not money; which may sound trite, but is worth a lot, even in money terms.

To get another angle on this, we asked Leslie Kirkley, the Director of Oxfam, to give us some idea of how much Oxfam aid went through Church and missionary channels. Some surprising facts emerged. When Oxfam started, he reckoned that 75% of grants went through Church channels. Even today, over half Oxfam projects (450 out of 812 in 1971) are with Christian agencies; and the value of this aid comprises more than 40% of Oxfam cash grants. In many of the other projects there is a priest in the background. In searching out suitable development agencies to work through, Kirkley says, 'our need has always been to find the group with integrity; in this way the missionary is far and away above any other group I've ever met.' Their integrity, their honesty, he says, even goes through to the local groups they've trained to succeed them. 'I can't remember even a case of diverting funds to the work of the Lord—which might be more tempting to them than outright dishonesty.' This compares well with more secular ventures such as co-operatives, which have all too often suffered from fingers in the till. 'Africa and India are littered with co-operative corpses.' The Catholics in particular combine a mixture of businesslike worldliness and motivation. 'Money only enables you to send people; the main need in Africa is people, it isn't money.' Where missionaries have faults, it is in sticking to large institutions and not being free to move into the newer fields such as mobile medicine; that and being 'cluttered up' with things 'like a guilt complex of a rich community towards a poor community'. Kirkley also found it 'embarrassing when they regard you as a tool of the Lord'.

From our much more limited experience we would go along with Kirkley about the quality of missionaries as aid workers.

We met a fair number of secular aid workers and whilst they almost all had the same intellectual attitudes to development as the missionaries—if slightly more radical—they seemed much less secure emotionally. We noticed a marked contrast when they came under conditions of hardship. Then it was more a case of count your problems than count your blessings. Young VSOs were much more easy going and tuned into the ways of today's world; they swore, they cracked a bottle of beer at the local bottle store, they roared round to African friends' homes on their scooters, they slept with the local girls. They were liked, but not particularly admired or respected, and it is anybody's guess which of these is more important in Africa today. They rose more to enthusiasm, and slumped more to depression. Older and more experienced secular aid workers had more staying power, but tended to have more preoccupation with salaries and living standards: a subject of conversation that was almost entirely missing amongst missionaries. We've often heard it said: 'It's all very well criticizing Christianity, but show me the humanist missionaries, show me the hospitals and the schools to equal the work of the Christian missions.' From what we've seen, there's justice in the jibe.

Even when we went to what has been regarded as a leader in a new style of secular project (Patrick Van Rensburg's Swaneng School at Serowe, Botswana) we were unimpressed. We were met with black looks by the Vice-Principal because we were late and had been unable to inform them because of a telephone breakdown. But discounting a surly welcome which we not once received from missionaries, the place was incredibly scruffy. Classrooms were dirty, papers were all over the floor, new paint-work and furniture was battered. The pupils were lounging around bored and the teachers seemed so involved in theories and opposition to 'élitism' (which as far as we could see had replaced the Devil in its powers to corrupt) that the place was at sixes and sevens. We happen to agree with most of the things that Swaneng stands for. But what we believed in theory and what we saw in practice were two different things. It seemed to us that the school, although bursting with ideas, seemed to lack the qualities missionaries have in plenty: dedication and the willingness to work. The abundant young teachers regarded their leisure time as 'theirs'. Going off to the local bar with the girls and affable youthful jocularity is one thing; but the place cried out for extra curricular activities and total involvement.

Quite a few missionaries in private said that they recognized that dedication and love were their strong points. Many mission or ex-mission hospitals were crowded when hospitals nearby had empty beds. But understandably they were loathe to crow about it. In a way, it is only the sort of thing that will be believed if it is said by outsiders. One missionary, not given to exaggeration or unkindness, described as 'the dregs of the medical profession' the secular aid staff recruited for the government hospital in which he was serving. 'One man had lost two jobs in the UK because he was schizophrenic.' The government concerned eventually fired all except the missionary. This was no doubt an exceptional case. But we heard many complaints about lack of concern, people unwilling to learn the language and to 'muck-in in a situation where doctors have to become anything from administrators to builders.

What we find quite incomprehensible is the fact that the missionary leadership back home fail to capitalize on this, their greatest asset and selling point. They even go out of their way to make life hard for themselves by underplaying the role of aid in missionary work.

Missionary societies, for example, are inordinately jealous of the success of Christian Aid, however much they may couch their jealousies in polite language. 'Christian Aid comes along,' Neville Cryer says, 'not talking about missionary aid but world development. After the first flush of co-operation the missionary societies discover that because Christian Aid is single minded it achieves a steadily increasing percentage of voluntary contributions. The Christian Aid directors have said they are part of Christian mission; but in practice, their appeals have come over virtually as a secular appeal for the underdog. This ties in and makes sense and the public says "Bang on!" It is this impact the missionary societies find so threatening. If it comes to a showdown the missionary societies must say, "If you talk of development only in material terms we must draw the line." I don't think the missionary societies have thought this through.'

Cryer at present heads the British and Foreign Bible Society and, as he was for four years Home Secretary of the Conference of British Missionary Societies, his words have weight.

Brian Rice, the Education Secretary of the Anglican USPG, said that it was the current fashion of Christians to concentrate too much on aid at the expense of the Gospel. 'The temptation to turn the stones into bread might well be called the Oxfam Temptation. Our Lord refused to do this. The real trouble of the Church in this country is that it has become a glorified social welfare organization which occasionally prays.' This was an oft-repeated sentiment. There may soon be a reversal of emphasis. 'People are sick of secular involvement,' said Canon Paul, now Warden of Lee Abbey in Devon, 'I hope it *won't* be a reaction, but I myself will be glad to see a stronger content of declarable Gospel.'

Other people said they thought Christian Aid had the best of it both ways: they got the money of church people out of loyalty because they were a Christian organization; and they got money from the public because they were 'practical': money didn't go on Church work or evangelism.

Alan Booth, the director of Christian Aid, said he did not see any wrong in Christians being in aid *per se*. 'I have often noticed that it was the two priests who passed by on the other side in the story of the Good Samaritan. Christ did not add the rider that all that was necessary to enter the Kingdom of Heaven was to love your neighbour then convert him. Christ did *not* say of the Samaritan, now tell him the Gospel. You don't have to justify doing good to people by adding the commercial.' Nor did he endorse any feeling that Christian Aid was more worth giving to than Oxfam because it was "Christian": 'I think this is wicked, to try and knock human generosity.' It was extremely important that Christian Aid organizations should be channels that participate in general aid programmes and not try to be special.

Booth was equally sure of the value of missionary societies. It was certainly true that some of them were not evolving fast enough. 'But you can't knock them. They were the way in which the simple common man participated in the Third World when the rich were preoccupied with building empires.' But they were working with tools that are out of date. 'It must be infuriating for this new organization, Christian Aid, to come in and swipe all the money. But the days when you could go out and preach the Gospel are long since past. You are talking from such a different culture. It's just not on. So the missionary society supports the

local church structure. We do that too. But the missionary societies are working more humbly and patiently within the structures
of the Third World, and we are tending to work on the frontiers
and margins, taking on economic development. The upbuilding
of the Church in the Third World, and the reviving of it from
Victorian embalment is as important as anything we do.'

We just can't see what bugs the missionary societies about aid.
The existence of Mother Teresas around the world, seems to give
the lie to the fact that aid and prayer, aid and the Gospel, can't
go together. Why get a hang up because you get a reputation for
being good at aid? No one we met in the secular field really
had any illusions about the ultimate objectives of missionary
organizations being the extension of Christianity. And if the
modern way of doing this is by service rather than preaching,
why worry?

Missionary pundits back in Britain seem, to us, virtually to do
a disservice to their men in the field by worrying incessantly
about theories, theologies and principles. If they put their noses
to the grind-stone and concentrated on doing two simple things:
raising money to send dedicated Christians overseas and project-
ing a clear image, one can't help thinking that their troubles
would evaporate.

CHAPTER THIRTEEN

The New Recruits

Has the missionary era ended? There are constant hairsplitting debates about this all over the missionary world. The trouble is that in addition to problems overseas, there are fewer and fewer recruits. The Catholics are suffering the most because going into an order is for life. The Protestants are compromising and accepting more and more people on short-term contracts.

In this chapter we describe a new scheme for short-term Catholic volunteers, which is meeting with great success, and some new Protestant recruits who give an indication of what future missionaries will be like. They are very different from missionaries even ten years their senior.

*   *   *

Robert and Jill de Berry are by no means typical of the new recruits we met at Selly Oak Colleges in Birmingham. But they will be more typical in a few years' time. They are a gay lively pair, both casually dressed. Robert is twenty-six, with hair you couldn't call 'long' but which is not short back and sides either. Jill, dressed in jeans, is twenty-three, bouncing and vivacious: she sat on the floor or with her feet tucked up on the chair. Between them they sported a clapped out old Morris Minor, hand-painted a two-tone green and decorated with stick-on flowers, little pink pigs and a Christian Aid poster of a corpse on a stretcher.

In a way, they represent the new kind of Livingstones. They emerge in the same tradition, from a good middle-class Christianity. Robert's father is rector of a well-to-do Oxford church. Jill's father is a managing director with ICI. Both came to missionary work after a considerable period of searching doubts, if not outright rebellion. 'I went to church,' said Jill, 'but anything to do with Christianity was dead for me. A dragging church service with a lot of middle-aged people. Services today are still a drag—but not in a lively church. Go into most churches and you'll face a lot of backs. Here at training college we have communion in a circle—this is round and total in itself.' She underwent a conversion experience before she met Robert. 'It's hard to explain. For a long time you don't relate, then you click.'

Robert went to public school, but very much noticed 'the clapped out dormobile among the Jags and Bentleys—a clergyman is always respected, but related to the ranks of "distressed gentlefolk".' At seventeen he faced his first real dilemma. 'There was the real Christianity of my parents. And the public school religion which was a bore and a bind. The main subject of conversation was homosexual sex. I was very anti-authority and mucked up one cadet course enough to be sent home.' He went on to university aiming to be an executive in British Rail; he loved transport. After university, he went overseas as a volunteer to Nigeria on an agricultural scheme. 'I made a complete mess of it. Every single thing went wrong. I tried to start a farm for school leavers. I tried to get land. All I did was get misunderstanding. The Minister of Agriculture came and all the Africans ran away. I was immensely depressed, and this gave me a sight of the failure of humanism. I got to a point of kneeling by my bed and sensed a great feeling of not needing to justify myself any longer. I didn't have to think in terms of grandiose successes. I came to trust in Christ. Things didn't go much better but I came to an understanding of myself.'

He decided to become an Anglican clergyman, and read modern theology. 'My absolute Christian religion was made relative. I began to see it in the setting of the times. Up to that point the Christian faith was absolutely right. Other people were absolutely wrong. And at a public school that was very comforting. Theology changed all that.'

It is not easy to see Robert and Jill fitting into the Church. They are too concerned with issues like world poverty to have a great deal of patience with bell-tower problems. Robert, in his first curacy, found it hard to see the justification of a £70,000 expenditure on a new cathedral close just so that the canons could be together. He sees many of the older clergy as a sad, tragic

problem: trapped in careers in which they now only half believe,
arid, dried up and unable to give. 'The biggest test of my faith
is not getting on with unbelievers, so much as getting on with my
fellow clergy. So many of them are utterly and completely lost.'

One of the attributes of the English parson seems to be his
droning intonation: you can often tell a clergyman on the
wireless two rooms away. You just *couldn't* put Robert in this
bracket, nor type Jill as the parson's wife. They are affable,
accepting, fun to be with. They are part of a growing number of
active young Christians who positively welcome the financial
difficulties facing the churches in this country. They see themselves
as forerunners of a minority Christianity; Christians in a post-
Christendom society. The sooner the essentials are separated
from the inessentials, the better it will be for Christianity.

*   *   *

The second young couple, Kevin and Penny Lawes, were also
Anglicans, but they were going out with the Methodist Missionary Society and training at a Baptist college. This alone would
have been impossible a few years ago. 'I think we are going to
shock a few people,' Penny told us. 'We are not of the same
world as the old missionaries and even of some of the younger
ones.' She likes the label missionary, but is also sure it's outdated.
'I really can't see that swearing or visiting pubs has much to do
with Christianity. I couldn't imagine us standing on a street
corner preaching in Brazil. I *can* see us talking to people over a
bar. Don't get me wrong,' she said, 'I don't think we go to one
in two weeks. But if missionary means anything it means keeping
your friends and staying normal.'

This 'staying normal' is a common theme amongst new
recruits. 'When we go home,' Kevin said, 'friends half expect
the worst. At half term they sort of said "But you're still the same."
We mean to keep it that way.'

They had certainly livened up the campus with their contribution to normality. When we met them Kevin was sporting a
green and pink stripped shirt, with tie to match. Penny was in a
simple midi skirt. The previous term she had been the stir of the
campus when she emerged in flaming red hot pants.

How did she get on with the conservative elements? 'The

fire-eating Baptists still come for training, but they get the corners
knocked off. So do we. Dialogue has just got to be on the cards.'

The de Berrys and the Lawes may or may not be typical of
the new Protestant missionaries. Perhaps what is important is
that they are accepted and they are of their own generation, as
the older ones were of theirs. Shortly after we met them we heard
of a Franciscan friar with flowing blond hair. He won't be the
only one.

When you bump into the missionaries of the future around the
world there will still be something of the oddball about them.
After all, it does sort you out from the crowd to enter missionary
training in this day and age. But at least the present generation
will be easy to relax with.

The training at Selly Oak matches the freshness of many of the
recruits. We were interested to see that all the missionary students,
for example, work in the grimmer areas of Birmingham on race
relations and community relations work, under the direction of
social workers. And they bring the face-to-face problems back
into the classroom. Here they argue through their decisions and
reactions. In lectures, reference back to this practical work is made
time and again. There is a predominant stress upon human
relationships, culture shock, cross-culture barriers and linguistic
difficulties.

To some, this 'encounter-teaching' does not go far enough.
But compared with the heavily theological syllabus five years ago
it is a major change.

Again, the syllabuses of the major denominations have now
merged: the Presbyterians, Anglicans, Methodists, Baptists,
and Congregationalists have pooled their resources.

David Lyon, the former Dean of Missionary Studies, has
brought in many of these changes. His syllabus reads like a text-
book on human understanding. He still complained that he felt
he'd achieved very little. Bringing in such sweeping reforms he
constantly had to make sure he wasn't going too fast for the
conservatives to swallow. Yet he was well aware that he must
push even harder to catch up with the changes of Asia and Africa.
His own thinking is way ahead of the syllabus.

He was still determined to push the practical subjects like
children's education out of the syllabus to squeeze in more time
for relationships and culture. Maintenance of land-rovers can be

mopped up by a bit of book-learning and experience overseas, he believes. But nothing would later correct an arrogant, unaware approach.

Some recruits, expecially the more conservative and the not so bright, were ruffled and puzzled by it all. The simple rules no longer held. As Penny Lawes put it, David Lyon was succeeding in 'knocking corners' off all of them.

★   ★   ★

Edwina Gately may fairly be said to represent all things new in the Catholic Church. She doesn't belong to an order: her self-chosen task has been to start a Voluntary Missionary Movement, and to call it by that name because she didn't want to sound like an institution or too holy. She wanted something modern. The significance of her work is that while recruits to the orders are dwindling she has a growing number of volunteers.

Unlike Protestants, who have sent lay missionaries overseas for 250 years, missionary work for Catholics was the prerogative of the priests and sisters. Edwina had to fight a two-year running battle to change this. She had to see everyone from the head of the Mill Hill Fathers to Cardinal Heenan, and she only won through in the end by brandishing Vatican II at every doubter. The documents of Vatican II have whole sections encouraging the laity to get stuck in, and she typed these quotations out on cards and quoted them wherever she went.

From the age of sixteen, Edwina was determined to be a volunteer teacher in Africa. She was turned down by VSO (which is wry in the light of what follows), but six weeks after she finished her training she went to Uganda. For a year she worked with the White Sisters at Musaka in a well-equipped, book-filled school. Then, champing at the bit, she asked the Bishop if she could take on something more demanding. 'I wanted something more, a chance of really contributing, and competing against greater odds.' The Bishop sent her to a school in the bush village of Kyamaganda. She was on her own. 'This was more the sort of thing I was thinking of,' she says. The 'school' was a barn-like building, and there were 68 girl boarders aged between eleven and seventeen who came from a radius of 100 miles around. The girls slept on the floor. The water came from a swamp.

There were three oil lamps between the whole school. They were three miles from the nearest road, and eighteen hitch-hiking miles to the nearest town. Edwina shared the same food as the girls—a diet of bananas and peanut sauce. She would go in on Saturdays to buy bacon and, as a special treat, sausages. She set to work and slowly built up or replaced her ancient equipment, maps and books (the Scripture textbooks were printed in 1867), writing letters all over the place. They put on a play, 'Cinderella' —African style, and made £62, 'which was an awful lot of money for us'. She had desks made by the local carpenters. She slept in the staff room, a basic whitewashed mud room. She got a dog, she says, 'so that I could speak English now and then. I was quite lonely. There were suddenly evenings when I had a yen to get dressed up and go to a dance.'

She coped, she says, because she is naturally confident, 'which is not necessarily a virtue', but it was a virtue there. She was never frightened: 'What was there to be frightened of?' But she did have several traumatic moments. There was the earthquake where she woke up and heard screams all around. 'All the kids— by then 150—started chanting the rosary, the last resort sort of thing. I went outside in my nightie. But all went quiet again. Then it started again, much much worse. Watching the ceiling I thought, 'it's going to fall on me, it's going to fall on me!' I should have been praying and all that, but all I could think was, how awful it would be to be found dead with my rollers in.' So she threw them off on the floor. 'Then I knew I *must* get out of the house in case it fell in. I've read of people who couldn't move but never really thought it happened. But I couldn't move a limb. Get out, you fool, get out, I said. A few houses had fallen down, but as you gather, I survived.'

After two years she had to leave. One morning she knew she was seriously ill. She couldn't even write properly, so she told the girls she'd be back in a day or two. She was delirious, and stayed in hospital a month, 'drugged to the eyeballs. My stomach was like a live aquarium because I'd been drinking swamp water.' The nuns told her that if she couldn't improve her living conditions she couldn't stay. The Bishop bought her a small fridge, but she knew it was time to come home and recuperate.

'I think it was Divine Providence,' she says with a grin, 'that the day after I hitched into hospital the King Freddy coup blocked

L

the roads. Had I left it another day I would never have got out because the people were out with spears and the roads were dug up.'

As she prepared to go back to Britain, she knew that the school would collapse unless she got more volunteers. She wrote to universities and teacher-training colleges and got three volunteers, two of whom went to work on a neighbouring school. Back in England she took up a teaching post in Liverpool and spent her time recruiting, writing articles and giving talks. Working entirely privately, she raised £800 and was able to send 28 teachers out as volunteers. But she was very dissatisfied with the vague training available, because conditions were so tough. 'I felt the Church itself should do something. Catholics have no lay missionary activity. It's been the preserve of priests and nuns. They have a very full training and are probably more religiously committed than I wanted. I wanted a *job*, but not as a catechist or preacher. When I looked around, we didn't have anything near the standard of the Protestants.'

Edwina knew from her experience that any new lay missionary body would have to be totally professional. In Uganda, she said, the people she recruited 'felt like appendages, outsiders'. But the missionary endeavour belongs to the whole Christian laity, she says. 'They should be working side by side with the priests, they should not be gap fillers.'

About this time the Vatican II documents came out, stressing the role of the laity. 'This was the support I needed for my ideas. I wrote articles, I drew up a draft of the kind of organization I needed. But I didn't get any kind of support.'

For two years she tried. She knocked on every possible door and hawked her idea around. It was a passion with her. She got pleasant murmerings and pats on the back for her good intentions, but no action. She went to see Bishop Ellis, the head of the Commission for Missionary Activity. She went to Cardinal Heenan, who said she should wait for guidance. She used to wake up having dreams about it; she was not going to take no for an answer, and she was determined that what she created would be central, within the Church, with the backing of the hierarchy.

At the end of two years, she gave up. Her bishop had invited her back to Uganda, and she went. After three months a letter

arrived from the Secretary of the Commission for Missionary
Activity telling her to come back. The seven major Catholic
missionary orders had got together; they wanted her to go ahead
and would give her complete freedom to create the organization
she wanted. They brought her to a damp, freezing house and
gave her an open cheque to furnish it. She did so the same afternoon from catalogues and did most of the redecorating herself.
She called the organization Voluntary Missionary *Movement*
because she didn't want a 'society' or 'organization'.

'I had a great deal of trouble with "Missionary" because of its
image, but I couldn't get rid of it. Apostle, the other suggestion,
was worse. To tone it down I put Volunteer in front.' She
advertised for volunteers, and within the first six months had
given 25 recruits a thorough training course and sent them on
their way. Now, two years later, a hundred people a year are
going out as a result of her efforts.

Her offices are a combination of efficiency and relaxing
comfort. There were big red paper poppies, clean red and white
furniture and pure white walls and book shelves. It all opened
on to a shady and intimate garden. There was an African gourd,
an African woven rug in black and white, African carvings and
shelves full of books on Africa, mostly new and definitely not
dusty. There was nothing lavish about the room; but it wasn't
pinch penny either. Edwina does not apologize for this. 'This
place is all I've got, although of course I don't own it; and when
the volunteers come back they love it. I remember one day a
local woman came to bring some pots and things and she was
horrified. She told people "They've got comfortable chairs and
a suite of furniture!" I could have murdered this woman.'
Edwina was scathing. 'What do they give? They go to church
and as a big effort they maybe even give fifty pence. They go
home to television, holidays. And they feel their fifty pence
is wasted because it's spent making life a bit easier when the
volunteers come back—"our money's going on an easy life!"
I'm in charge of 100 personnel and I have one part-time secretary
to help handle a hundred letters a week. If I didn't know I could
put my feet up . . . why the hell shouldn't it be! Why shouldn't
we be smart and have nice things? My job is not a nine-to-five
thing; for me it's 24 hours. It may be waiting at the airport at
midnight. I have very few holidays; I'm never free to go off.'

She feels the same about her missionaries in Africa. They may have desperately little money. But if the money is there—take it and use it, that's what it's for. 'I like them to enjoy themselves, to have books and things.' They should dress properly, and look smart. In general, they should not 'go native', which can be patronizing. 'To some it comes naturally; it did to me. But you can't try to do it. You can get disillusioned if you want to identify—you must start with a decent standard. You can even set an example in a poor little house with white-washed walls, local matting and a few bookshelves. Beauty is basic. It's a sad thing that convents have thought it a virtue to deny themselves beauty. in depriving themselves they've deprived others.'

Edwina sees a very different role for the missionaries she is sending out. Their main function is to release the priest from the practical work of building or running schools or hospitals. A lot of recruits are apprehensive: ' "Will I have to teach religion?" ' To others it is a wholly new idea to be missionaries. 'I try to get recruits to say why they are voluntary missionaries before they are dismissed as "missionaries". I think the work of missions is undersold; that there is a terrible lack of publicity. I've spent several years of my life in this and I know what it's like to be an oddity, a figure of fun if you like. Or even worse it makes me a walking saint. If I said I was a nurse people wouldn't blink. People think of us as "all that hard work". You should come to our parties. You'd see!'

The breadth of the new thinking in the organization can be seen in the careful and thorough training. Almost 50 lectures cover African traditional religions, the Christian attitude to revolution and violence, African values, African socialism, health and hygiene, the relationships between rich and poor countries, as well as a thorough coverage of all things pertaining to Christian missions. Evening film shows include a wide range of concern, from repeats of 'Cathy Come Home' to satirical cartoons from Czechoslovakia. The courses take place in an old converted warehouse near the Mill Hill Fathers, who spent thousands on it. ('That's co-operation,' says Edwina.)

The volunteers who train together do their best to keep in touch afterwards; and VMM encourages this through newsletters. Glancing through these, you get the impression of a young and affable crowd. There is a subdued but strong idealism, but it is an idealism of deeds rather than words. Significantly, the heroine of VMM—at least if their prayers are anything to go by—is Mother Teresa, whose sayings, prayers and poetry far outnumber all others in the training manual. 'The biggest disease today,' one of the Mother Teresa quotes goes, 'is not leprosy or tuberculosis, but rather the feeling of being unwanted, uncared for and deserted by everybody. The greatest evil is the lack of love and charity, the terrible indifference towards one's neighbour who lives at the roadside assaulted by exploitation, corruption, poverty and disease.'

CHAPTER FOURTEEN

The Crunch Issues

Missionary societies have a sticky future; the writing is on the wall in all sorts of ways. Incomes are static, or declining. Where this is not so, inflation cancels out the gains. Recruitment has tailed away and no longer meets natural wastage from death or resignation. Even more important, missionaries face a crisis of identity. Independence has pushed them off the centre of the stage; and working in the wings makes it hard to carve out a clear role for themselves. This makes it doubly difficult to present a clear unequivocal image to their supporters. And so the troubles go full circle, with fewer recruits and fund-raising difficulties as a result.

Let's take, to start with, the actual role missionaries are performing because much flows from this. It will already have been apparent that very few missionaries are performing tasks which are obviously 'missionary'. 'The first step to recognize', said Bishop Stephen Neill in the *Church of England Newspaper* in November 1970, 'is that the great majority of those who are called missionaries today are not doing and never have done any missionary work in their lives. I describe a missionary', Bishop Neill went on, 'as a man or woman possessed by an intense sense of call to proclaim the Gospel of Christ where, apart from the presence of the missionary, there would be no proclamation of that Gospel at all.' On his terminology, there are very few missionaries around today. There are people involved in what he calls 'Church extension' like the Christian Industrial Training Centres in Kenya. There are people involved mostly in what he calls 'Inter-Church Assistance' helping in clerical training programmes. But missionary work as such hardly exists, and what does exist is being done by indigenous Christians rather than by expatriates. For this reason, he says, there should be no need for the interposition of a missionary society between the old and new churches. The local churches, or a central ecumenical body, like the All Africa Conference of Churches, should make all appointments. Missionary societies could perhaps help by acting as recruiting agencies for Church workers, looking after their interests and retirement; but for the rest he thinks they should go back to their calling and concentrate on real missionary work, going to far-off lands like Nepal and Cambodia.

To some Bishop Neill's ideas will sound like a clarion call; a clearing of the decks for a return to first principles. But John Taylor thinks that the reality is a great deal more complicated than this. In a reply in the same paper a week later, he stressed this: 'Any thinking which preserves the old distinctions between Christian and non-Christian countries, domestic and foreign, home missions and overseas missions, is liable to be out of date and to distort the truth.' Furthermore, 'the more one looks at the new opportunities of proclaiming Christ in the world today, the more impossible it becomes to draw such a line as Bishop Neill proposes between Church extension and his fourth category which alone he calls "misionary work".' Bishop Neill's Church-centred presentation of mission does not, Taylor went on, seem to take account of the growing number of missionaries who are 'called to a strictly lay apostolate in some secular employment overseas. The whole point of their being there is to take the Gospel where they cannot take the Church as such.'

All this revolves around the semantics of the words mission, missionary, and Gospel. Everybody we met read their own personal convictions into these words. They are so loaded that they are hard to use, but an increasing number of committed Christians of all persuasions see their Christianity in terms of living the Christian Gospel, rather than preaching it. They may or may not go so far as to do without preaching, but they certainly soft pedal the subject. The reasons for this are manifold: the theological crisis, the increasing respect for the complexities of human relationships and other cultures, and the shift away from authoritarianism. People would tell us when we discussed the concept of a missionary that every Christian is a missionary and is engaged in the universal mission of the Church. This may be theologically sound—that a man from Leicester who goes to London to preach Christianity is a missionary; but he would get

a funny reaction if that's how he described himself to the
Londoners. To the overwhelming majority of the public, a
missionary is someone who is sent by a group of believers to
another country to propound his beliefs.

Taking the broader conception, missionaries still exist in large
numbers. It is only the method and expression of belief that has
altered. Precisely because developing countries now have flourish-
ing indigenous churches, the need for people within the existing
church structures is diminishing. But the opportunities of other
kinds of Christian service are if anything growing.

Not everyone can adjust to the new roles. 'In the past everything we've done has been with a brass band and labels,' Colin
Morris said; 'It requires a certain humility to recognize that some
of the other mob have an element of truth.' Nor have the new
attitudes necessarily percolated through even to the African or
Asian Christians. Many missionaries told us that the label
'missionary' was useful because it meant immediate acceptance
by the local church.

The changing concepts have also called for a more exacting
kind of Christianity-in-the-market-place. As the great missionary institutions have passed more and more to government
control, some missionaries have found it hard to make the
distinctively 'Christian' contribution they originally envisaged
for their lives. When you serve in a government set-up, one
doctor said, 'it is difficult to live a distinctively Christian life.
In a Christian hospital you can insist on ideals of service in
teaching and medical service which you believe to be right.
If people don't live up to this you are in a position to insist—you
can change the staff. In government situations you can't.'

The missionary policy makers face the same problems but on
a wider scale. It is easier to have it your own way in a 'Christian'
set up, but more challenging, frustrating, and complex to carry
your Christianity into the heart of the secular world. According
to the Africa Secretary of CMS this is the biggest single issue.
'The Church is in danger of being a spectator, watching from the
touchline the main arena in which the life of this world is being
lived and where history is being made. If this issue can be faced
fearlessly, a period of exciting new advance is before us. What is
needed is a reassessment of work in terms of penetration into the
world with the Gospel.'

The Society of Friends (Quakers) is one of the early runners in this field of moving into the secular world. They dropped the word 'missionary' from their overseas work way back in the nineteen-twenties, and having no priesthood were naturally anxious to ensure that their overseas efforts were in the non-church world. In the 'thirties, 'forties and 'fifties they were most known for their refugee and relief programmes, but of late the Friends' Service Council has been concentrating on practical peacemaking. They have made their buildings available, at the UN, in the Middle East and elsewhere, as neutral meeting places where diplomats from opposing camps could meet without publicity or pressure. This concerned, knowledgeable but unpartisan witness of individual Quakers has made its mark.

In the Catholic world, the move towards secular rather than Church-structured missionary work has taken place in organizations like the volunteer programme of the Catholic Institution for International Relations, and in Edwina Gately's Voluntary Missionary Movement. In addition, individual Catholics have increasingly gone out with secular aid organizations.

If the trend continues, it may well be that missionary organizations will become clearing houses for Christians who simply want to serve in the developing world. If 'life service' becomes the exception, which has already happened in Protestant societies, then inevitably missionary societies will become glorified employment agencies.

They will never be purely this, because traditionally they have developed an institutional life of their own. Membership of one of the large societies is like membership of a good club: it opens doors and provides contacts. 'You have a network of friends. We could stay with families all over the world.' Others stressed the feeling that people were behind them: 'You are supported in everything from feeling depressed to needing a new cooker.' Several people emphasized that the only practical difference between being a 'missionary' and going out through the Overseas Development Ministry was in the personal back up. 'I look on the missionary society for a sense of community more than anything else' and 'The missionary side is for our own personal help. It doesn't mean we're any better at our jobs.'

If this trend does continue, we would hope that three distinctive features of present-day missionary societies are not lost. The first of these is training. There is no doubt whatsoever that as *institutions* the missionary societies are a great deal more thorough in their training than any government, Oxfam or VSO programme. Recruits undergo from six months to several years full-time study, and as a result the men and women are generally more balanced, more knowledgeable about language and culture, and more ready for conflict and stress than any two-year government contract people. The second distinctive quality of the missionary societies is that they are more supportive than any secular agency we know. They really do seem to care if John Smith in Addis Ababa has a stomach bug. They really do seem to care if he is under stress or can't face up to his job.

Attractive to us as outsiders, was the fact that this caring was totally unrelated to success. There was no profit motive; and much more subtle, there was no judgement of success in bricks and mortar terms. It didn't matter that one man was a brilliant surgeon and another was a slightly bumbling social worker. We noticed the little things—that people always asked after your children, or what you were doing. They knew of each other's hopes, failures, and personal quirks. Even though scattered by thousands of miles, they remained a living community.

The third quality we valued about missionary societies was that this caring did not cease when the temporary usefulness of someone ceased. People did not go into limbo, forgotten, when they ceased to be 'overseas missionaries'. This even happened to us as outsiders. Long after we had finished our contract as researchers with the Church Missionary Society, individual executives at the head office, and individual missionaries overseas, kept in touch. They had no reason to; but it was an attention to human beings that did not pass unnoticed.

*   *   *

If missionary societies are changing by the minute, their supporters don't yet know it. One senior executive in one of the biggest societies said he thought the mental time gap between the leaders and their supporters was fifty years. He didn't add that maybe some of the societies are almost happy to keep it that way.

The old missionary image, after all, was a comforting one. Although Christianity was having a tough time in Britain, it was nice to know, as John Taylor puts it, 'that somewhere the other side of the world there was a Shangri La where it really worked'. Our Elsie could go and do good work and people would actually listen. There was somewhere where miracles really did happen. The primitive natives fitted the bill. They were respectful, and keen to acquire the blessings the missionaries brought—health, education, jobs, and the white man's religion which was bound up with these things. There were occasional rebellions—which added to the glory by providing a sprinkling of martyrs but missionaries were never—*horrible* thought—ignored. If you gave money to missions, things *happened*. You were not propping up old structures in Britain, you were advancing God's Kingdom. All the early literature proclaimed in stirring and often military terms the glories of the Lord's battles.

Consciously or otherwise, missionary societies projected a myth. One missionary now in his forties told us: 'Next to God this was it! There was definitely this feeling that if you really wanted to be a grade I Christian you had to go overseas. And here I was, consorting with the archangels.' Missionaries may well be moving into the secular world, but there is still this *feeling* that they are bringing down converts like clay pigeons. A missionary music teacher once addressed an English audience and described a normal week's work. She told them of the singing club, the glee club of music appreciation, violin recitals, of learning to make and appreciate indigenous music. At the end of her talk an old soul asked, 'Yes dear—but when do you have time to do your *missionary* work?'

The real fear of the societies is that if they stressed that miracles don't happen there, any more than they do here, they would lose support.

The most sensitive issue is probably race. It was one thing a few years ago to send money to build hospitals for the natives in far off Africa. Now coloured people are here in our midst, embarrassingly so. Recently the major Protestant societies commissioned a market research report into attitudes to missionary work. The majority of missionary supporters were found to believe that immigration into Britain was a bad thing.

The difficulties here are obvious. The Rev. Colin Charlton, a missionary society area secretary, said that immigration had already had an adverse effect on financial support, and the situation would get worse if societies spoke out. He felt they should be outspoken even if it did lose them money. 'I have been attacked on the church steps many times,' he told us. On one occasion a bowler hatted businessman came up after a race relations talk: 'So you're for the bloody blacks, are you?' he said as he passed. At the time of the Middle East Six-Day War Charlton preached on the necessity of exercising patience and grace in a situation fraught with political difficulties. 'Have you been in the Middle East?' the local church warden asked. 'Those wogs are impossible to deal with. And the Gyppos are worse.' Once Charlton preached on the text 'Other sheep I have that are not of this fold', and the need for Christians to build bridges of friendship with immigrants, saying 'If we don't, who will?' He was besieged on the steps by a keen evangelical with a Scripture Union badge who objected strongly that immigrants in any way belong in England. This Bible enthusiast had conducted a survey in his office and found 87% wanted all immigrants sent home, and wanted legislation to force immigrants to live and dress like the English. Charlton was reminded of the African dance troupe touring the USA bare breasted who were told to cover up to meet the local convention. 'All right,' they were reputed to have said. 'We trust American ladies will go along with the opposite convention when they visit our country.'

At present he says, missionary work is sold in middle-class terms to the old and ailing. 'It's like a great big geriatric unit here. Look around you.' And whilst there is growing dissatisfaction with the Afro-Asian bloc amongst the old, the young look at the world and say they want to serve. So Christian Aid and Oxfam get support which previously went to missionary societies, and this is more serious than people presume. 'I don't think young people see anything distinctive in what we stand for. For distinctive read Christian.'

'Let me tell you about a meeting I attended in Colchester. As you approach you see a sign "Camulodum: Britain's oldest town". The missionary meeting was attended by the oldest inhabitants, 40 people, 39 of them women. The aggregate of the ages must have been nearly 3,000 years. The slides were half projected on the screen and half on the wall. Every slide was out of focus. The missionary had retired some time ago, twenty-five years I should think. And she was very deaf. Questions had to be relayed across the room, courtroom fashion. At some point in the proceedings some woman got up and sang "Ten Thousand Sparkling Rills" to a battered church-hall piano played by a person who had obviously never before accompanied the singer. I took a teenager with a guitar with me and this kid was shattered that this should be perpetrated in the name of missionary work.'

Charlton uses a team of young people and tackles the issues head on. 'We tackled race relations at a meeting in Watford, for example. I introduced the meeting with a bit of humour, relating the story of a man who told me over lunch that Malcolm Muggeridge and Enoch Powell were the two greatest living Englishmen. A chap at the back said "Hear, hear". I thought, we're in for a good night here. We sang "Our Town" and "These Different from Us". These tend to get racialists incensed. One of the youngsters spoke on the necessity of exercising caring in respect of immigrants. It was obvious that this chap at the back was getting more and more irate. At coffee time I decided to leave it to the kids. He made a beeline for the youngsters. One of the girls slew him. She knew her facts. His unreasonable prejudice was shattered by fact and conviction. A youngster without tact was far better than a professional like me. This, to me, makes missionary work interesting. They won't forget *that* meeting in a hurry. I'm a bit bloody minded. But there are too many angry young men and not enough angry young Christians. We have every right to thunder it.'

These problems have been brewing for a long time: we were intrigued that Roland Allen writing on 'Missionary Methods' over forty years ago had this to say:

> We have allowed racial and religious pride to direct our attitude towards those whom we have been wont to call 'poor heathen'. We have approached them as superior beings, moved by charity to impart of our wealth to destitute and perishing souls. We have used that argument at home to wring grudging and pitiful doles for the propagation of our faith. . . We have been anxious to do something for them. And we have done much. We have done everything for them. We have taught them, baptized them, shepherded them. We have managed their funds, ordered their services, built their churches, provided their teachers. We have nursed them, fed them, doctored them. We have trained them, and have even ordained some of them. We have done everything

for them, but very little with them. We have done everything for them except give place to them. We have treated them as 'dear children', but not as 'brethren'.[1]

The missionary chickens have now come home to roost, and one suspects that the societies are going to pay dearly. To be fair to them, the overseas workers did wake up to the sins of paternalism long before their counterparts in business and colonial affairs. The Catholics have been training African priests all this century, and the Anglicans had devolved power to the Nigerian Church, for instance, years before independence was on the cards. Some may have been token transfers, but any reading of the facts shows that missionaries were ahead of all thinking except that of the nationalists and left wing. But if they woke up to the facts overseas they certainly didn't transmit their thoughts to their supporters at home.

Another reason for the huge divide between home supporters and the realities overseas may be the structure of missionary societies. Again we quote Roland Allen:

> Missionary societies began their crusade not by striving to call out the spirit of Christian men whose occupation carried them abroad, not by trying to impress upon the Church at home that Christ calls all his people to witness for Him wherever they may be, wherever they may go, but by creating an army of professional missionaries. The whole system of secretaries, boards, offices, accounts, contracts with missionaries, statistical returns, reports, reeks of it.[2]

The Methodists have avoided the worst pitfalls: the Methodist Missionary Society is an inherent part of the whole Methodist Church, not a separate body. Their little magazine *Now*, by far the best of the missionary magazines, feels quite free to rove over any issue of Christian outreach—in this country or overseas. Mission for them is one, and this is not just a pious theological hope. This theme of 'Mission is one' kept recurring among missionary leaders, but they admit that 'It's only recently that the Church has felt mission is not a pious extra, but something necessary for the whole Church. . .'

[1] *Missionary Methods*, Roland Allen, Lutterworth Press, 1968.
[2] *Ibid.*

'The whole organization of every missionary society,' another told us, 'was designed to do one thing: to raise the cash to pay a man to go and be a missionary "there". This is terribly obvious, but with a few exceptions, they haven't realized that their entire structure is incongruous. Their way of operating just isn't on. I'm cynical enough to think that the reason USPG and the Methodists are gallivanting into Latin America is because Latin America is one of the few areas of the world where you can go in this fashion.'

The Home Secretaries of the societies are notoriously conservative because they know only too well where their support lies. If the archetypal church supporter is middle aged, the average missionary supporter is even older. Four out of five missionary supporters are over thirty-five, and half are fifty-five or over. Missionary societies are ageing institutions in a time of rapid change overseas. No wonder there is a gulf. Max Warren, former General Secretary of CMS, once said that as missionaries were part of a revolutionary movement, he looked forward to the time when there would be bricks thrown through the windows by an angry public. But as far as we can see the glass is safe enough.

*　　*　　*

When we came back to Britain after touring missionary projects for several months, we were still pretty impressed. But our enthusiasm took a hard knock as we went about gathering material on the home front. If missionary societies have got an old-fashioned image, then from what we saw in many of the offices in London, they deserve it. One chief executive told us that when he moved into his job the furniture in his office had been unchanged for eighty years. He threw the lot out, cut the huge office in half, brought down the height of the ceiling, and got himself a new desk and fittings. 'Don't like it,' his predecessor warned on visiting. 'Not dignified. It doesn't command the respect that goes with the position.'

Missionary society headquarters are amiable enough places, but they do not give out an air of efficiency. Perhaps this is again because they are too kind. 'There are no penalties for failure,' one member of an executive committee told us. 'In industry the power thing is understood. Here it's not.' In consequence, retired missionaries and people past their dotage are kept on in jobs they have ceased to hold down. Personally, we found this a welcome contrast to the ruthlessness of the world outside. It may not satisfy the time and motion chaps, but the fact that people consider other human beings makes up for a lot.

The real disaster is the failure to put across their story. 'If missionary societies could produce a clear definition of what mission is all about I am sure they could produce as much money as before,' Dr. Hinchcliffe, in charge of mission at Church House, told us. We'd go along with that. The archaic literature the societies send to their supporters is a travesty of the work we saw in Africa. It is couched in 'church' language, a sort of religious esperanto that you will never hear at bus stops. When missionaries in Africa talked to us about their work, their hopes, and their failures they did not use this language: and yet they communicated. But in their prayer letters they often went over to this special, precious kind of language; and the societies faithfully passed this rarefied stuff on to the supporters.

The literature presents a stultifying 'goodness'. You will seldom find real controversy, anger, real human failure or anything the slightest bit 'naughty'. They all know this. Gwen Evans, editing our earlier document In Search of the Missionary,[1] told us what a refreshing change it was to be able to handle such stuff without exercising an eagle eye for what might offend. Even the word 'bloody' got through. Sometimes the sins of omission are downright dishonest. Catholic write-ups of Edwina Gately's fight to establish the Voluntary Missionary Movement made no reference at all to the total failure of the hierarchy to give early backing to the project, merely making passing references to 'frustrations'. Any gutsy material was automatically cut to preserve the image.

When we were writing off to all the missionary societies for their literature, we used to get the post in the mornings and sometimes had to smile at the quaintness of it. And it's not because we are unsympathetic. It just seemed so incredible that in this day and age people were still turning out such archaic material. We appreciate that, as Canon Paton put it

[1] Published by The Highway Press, 1970.

to us; 'The bumph is worse than the reality. In among the holier than thou brigade you will find people you really like.' This is true. But most missionary supporters in Newcastle-upon-Tyne do not meet the leaders. They see the literature; and if they are old they are reassured that somewhere on this muddled world, saints are still at work. If they are young they presumably laugh, or go their ways and write off all things missionary.

This is all so sad, because the reality would make good press and TV material. Summed up in one selling message they could communicate. 'Whereas Oxfam and the rest raise money for the tractors, we do something even more important. We send dedicated men who care.'

There is no real drive or dynamism in promotion on the home front. In total, the Protestant missionary societies have an aggregate income that exceeds the income of Oxfam and Christian Aid: you would not think so, from the impact they make. Part of the reason for this is an other-worldliness; a desire for really committed prayer-backed support. One young missionary put it this way, in a letter to us:

> As I go around various churches in the next few months talking about my work in Africa I will show slides illustrating the terrible poverty and suffering. Now I could play on guilt feelings and tell congregations what they ought to do in pretty strong terms. This will probably result in a reasonable collection, they will certainly think they have given generously, but then home they will go to their comfortable homes and forget until the next missionary anniversary. No, this is not good enough. I'm working in Africa not because I feel I *ought* to be there (such people are a pain in the buttock); I'm there because I *want* to be there. . . As I talk to audiences I shall preach Christianity, as the Church understands it, because if I can get just *one* person in each meeting to become a 'dedicated Christian', to live a sacrificial life for the rest of his or her life then I will achieve more than using the £10 collection given out of guilt. I want money to be given willingly, joyfully and not reluctantly and the dedicated Christian does just this and gives not only of his abundance either.

We sympathize with this attitude. But nobody would deny the Salvation Army is dedicated: yet they are not averse to banging the drum and raising money from the devil himself. So, too, with Christian Aid. They have dedicated Christians who

M

contribute money; it doesn't stop them collecting money from the rest. Missionary societies almost seem to go out of their way to avoid the filthy stuff. 'To be honest,' one area secretary told us 'I talk very little about money. I talk about people at the other end. Some in darkness, some not so much so. In all the donkeys' years I've been doing it I've rarely talked about money.' How, then, did he measure his effectiveness? 'I've never thought of it.' He admitted TV was making great inroads into audiences, and wished he knew the answer. 'Sometimes you get three or four people, but that doesn't worry you. I never count heads.' He was a sweet, gentle man. We were not surprised when he told us many of the clergy he visited regarded him as a confidant, a personal friend to whom a man could unload; but we were vaguely surprised when told that he regarded this as 'a big slice of his job'.

We were surprised to see that most missionary societies do not maintain the first elements of the promotional structure that would be deemed standard to almost any modern British charity. If a donor sent £5 that was the end of the matter in some cases; he wasn't even placed on a register of donors, or mailed in subsequent years. Very little emphasis was given to covenants, a uniquely effective British taxation device that raises tens of millions of pounds a year for other charities. Very little was being done to up-date the traditional silver coin in the plate; with the inevitable result that average giving remains at a few pence a year. A quarter of churchgoers make no separate donation to a missionary society and another third give no more than 50p a year. Only one in five supporters gives more than £2. Sacrificial giving exists, with people giving till it hurts, but there is a great makeweight of other church supporters who get off very lightly, but who would give a lot more if asked in the right way.

Bernard Llewellyn at Oxfam always used to say he had little patience with small Catholic missions who frequently wrote in to Oxfam saying 'We went ahead in faith, now we are broke and we are sure you will provide.' God presumably loves prudent accountants, he used to say, as well as saints. In like vein, God presumably loves good publicists as much as He loves those who wait around for the Holy Spirit to do the donkey work. But the suspicion of brashness, of too much order, of too much organiza-

tion remains. And so the organizations are sinking deeper and
deeper into financial trouble.

★   ★   ★

One of the important issues for the future is the existence of so
many different competing missionary societies. There are, in this
country, ten different Anglican missionary societies, at least as
many Catholic missionary orders, a society each for the Baptists, Congregationalists, Methodists, Episcopalians, Friends and
Presbyterians, plus a dozen or more others—some interdeno-
minational.

There are obvious advantages in diversity. People have their
fierce and passionate loyalties to particular traditions: 'all missionary society people know in their bones that they are minorities.
If it comes to a crunch they think they'll lose out in any merger.'
There are similar suspicions against any ideas for bringing the
independent missionary bodies back within the control of the
Church. Sir Kenneth Grubb perhaps best states the classic position:

> I suspect that if the Church of England were its own missionary
> society today, if missions became a single and official Board of the
> Church, much useful flexibility, inspiration and initiative would
> be lost. Whenever general economies should be demanded, one
> may guess that missions would suffer first. In this whole line of
> argument there is a good measure of bureaucratic power-seeking,
> an urge for centralisation for its own sake and not for the sake of
> 'fields ripe unto the harvest'. The Church of England is a noble and
> nice body, but it does not strike me with irresistible force as an
> enterprising or an enthusiastic one, ready to spend and be spent
> in the worldwide extension of the Kingdom of God.[1]

The real issue is not wholesale mergers within a monolith.
It is rationalization. There is no reason why the societies cannot
use the same marketing and finance service. It is generally
acknowledged that missionary societies—all of them—present a
poor public image. There is widespread misunderstanding of their
role, a huge educational updating task to be tackled. Why on
earth not do it together? If they could find agreement to set
aside as little as 2 per cent of their joint incomes for this they

[1] Sir Kenneth Grubb, K.C.M.G., *Crypts of Power*, Hodder & Stoughton,
1971.

would have a kitty of well over £100,000 to play with. And this, in professional hands, would do a lot to right the problem. So, too, with fund raising. Can anyone doubt that the phenomenal growth of Christian Aid in recent years (40 per cent in one year) is due to the promotional power of working together on a single cause? Suppose the missionary societies were to come together for two joint fund-raising events a year, including a 'mission week', would this not give them the promotional power they now lack? This need not lead to any diminution of existing incomes: what they do together as distinct from what they do apart should be a bonus, perhaps gradually growing as they learn to work together. As Neville Cryer, the head of the Bible Society, said to us, 'The question should not be, what can we do together, but rather what are the distinctive things we *can't* do together.' Cryer believes a common magazine would be a binding force, as would a joint radio and TV public relations unit.

Apart from growing financial pressures, there is quite a strong public pressure for greater co-operation or amalgamation. Clergy often express their resentment at the number of approaches they get for money from different missionary causes. Market research threw up the fact that two-thirds of clergy and well over half the missionary supporters would favour fewer societies. Partly as a result of this, talks have been going on between USPG and the Methodists; between CMS, Bible Churchman's Missionary Society and the South American Missionary Society; and between the Jerusalem and the East Society and the Mission to the Jews. Whether it will ever lead to anything is anybody's guess. One man at Church House was not hopeful. 'Several societies have merged in USPG and they have disappeared without trace. Mention "Let's merge" and you don't see the other societies for dust.'

★   ★   ★

It is not surprising that another crunch issue is at least making mission *look* a two-way process. One of the commonest attitudes of the man in the street on hearing that missionaries still exist is that we have got a nerve sending missionaries from a Britain that is anything but Christian. This was also the attitude of a number of Africans we met. It is obviously a very fair question.

There is already a certain amount of two-way missionary work going on. There are Japanese Christian missionaries in Nepal, and Japanese missionary doctors in Thailand. There are Southern Indian Christians and Koreans working as missionaries in North India, Tamil missionaries in Singapore and Indian missionaries in Ethiopia. There are even occasional missionaries who come to this country. In 1970 a Persian came as a curate to Blackpool and an Indian evangelist came to York and Cambridge, but it hardly produced understanding: 'Oh yes, he's come to work among foreign students' was the usual reaction. Lawi Imathiu (Chapter 10) whom we had met in Kenya was one of these new missionaries. He had similar experiences at Cambridge, which came as a complete shock to him. But, undaunted, he had returned to Kenya and set up his own missionary venture. The Boran tribe had lost three-quarters of their cattle in the Shifta rebellion, together with many of their menfolk. Lawi had had reports from one of his evangelists who had travelled 300 miles through the troubled area. He pressed for and got famine relief together with a deliberate government policy of reconciliation. Then he got together all the Meru tribeswomen and explained the needs of the Boran. The women, who were poor themselves, set out to give 1,000 new sets of children's clothes. Still not satisfied, he got together with his agricultural officer and planned an extensive programme of resettlement using young VSO volunteers.

If missionary societies really meant their work to be two way, they would put money into projects like this in a way that has not yet happened. To be sure, CMS puts aside £15,000 a year in a special 'Frontier' fund and this is largely expended in supporting evangelists of the newer churches tackling pioneer work. CMS also created something of a stir in 1970 by announcing that for the first time it intended to branch out into work amongst immigrants in Britain, and leading thinkers within CMS talk about using their residential retreat 'Foxbury' as a base for a multi-national team of evangelists to work in Britain. The British and Foreign Bible Society has devolved all its translation work to an international society, the United Bible Society, on which only one of seven executives is British. And the Overseas Missionary Fellowship, has been fully internationalized for some years.

The Roman Catholics have never had quite the same imperialist and Western associations as those that have bedevilled Protestant missions. The Anglican Church in particular had close connections with the colonial leaders, and the fact that Catholics looked to Rome rather than London has been a decided advantage. But even so, there is little evidence of black–white internationalism in their missionary set-ups. It is still a case of Irish, British, Italian and European priests and nuns going out to do missionary work, and this balance must shift radically if any real credence is to be given to the theme 'mission is one'. It still seems to outsiders that two-way mission is the 'in-thing' to profess. It is a pious intention that all proper thinking theologians and missionary leaders will endorse; but there is little sign of action.

If missionary societies meant business in this field, then they would do two things. They would make money available in large amounts for missionary work by the newer churches. And they would invite really significant numbers of missionaries here from these churches.

There is no doubt in our minds that African Christians have qualities of simple saintliness that would be salutary for British audiences. They may not have the book learning, they may not be versed in the sophistries of the West, but they exude a visible Christianity much lacking in Britain. We think of men like Bishop Hilary who replaced Trevor Huddleston in Masasi; a gentle, wonderful man. There would undoubtedly be huge problems. The supporters, as we have indicated earlier in this chapter, may be quite willing to pay for someone in Britain to go and do work in India; they may be wholly unwilling to get the better bargain of two trained Indians for the same money. And it may be all very well to bring saintly African Christians to England: but how long would they retain their St. Francis qualities in this brash and avaricious society?

But can anyone really think that 99 per cent white organizations sending missionaries to 99 per cent coloured countries in a one-way exchange is really what 'mission' should be about in the mid-twentieth century?

*　　*　　*

Even if Western missionary organizations mend their ways it is debatable whether they will ever undo the damage of past paternalism. The past errors of the Church are too thick on the ground. Professor Mbiti of Kampala, in his eloquent little pamphlet *The Crisis of Mission in Africa* says:

> The Church in Africa is suffering from a conservatism which makes it look like a relic of medieval European Christianity deposited here and left to rust and rot away. Nowhere did our Lord Jesus give us a rigid Christianity which cannot be changed. We are sticking too firmly to the rules and regulations, structures and traditions which have come to us through Western Churchmanship. This Churchmanship is, hopefully, beginning to change even in Europe and America and we are doing diservice to our Faith by sticking so tenaciously to all the anachronisms, mistakes, rigidity and traditions.

He says the Church in Africa has become like 'a toothless child which eats pre-chewed food from its mother's mouth; the Church has to produce a Christianity with the imprint MADE IN AFRICA, not a cheap imitation of the Christianity of earlier periods.' That the age of foreign missions in Africa is now over is a fact, he says. 'We can neither weep over it nor rejoice about it.' But it does pose immense problems. Although the foreign missions have vacated all the seats of power, they have left behind them the paraphernalia which neither preserves the best of the West nor develops the possibilities of emerging Africa.

What do we give to Christendom, Professor Mbiti asked, 'if we only speak in a foreign language, if we only open our mouths to repeat imported hymns, if we stretch out our hands only to beg for foreign aid in the Church, if we get on our feet only to pursue ready-made structures which don't speak to our peoples? We have mastered Latin and Greek, Hebrew and English, we have mastered Romanism, Canterburysm, Athenism and Genevanism: can't we also speak Africanism in the Church?'

The conservatism in the African churches obviously goes back deep into the roots of tribal society. One Ugandan clergyman told us that even though he was forty-three his father still did not think he was old enough to hold a leading position in the Church. It is hard to see this changing when most developing countries are going through major class struggles in which the conservative groups will lose out.

The Christian Church in China lost out because it slavishly

adopted so much that was obviously Western. Canon Paton, writing in 1953, pointed out that almost everything the missionaries had done was at one remove from the moving forces in Chinese society. They had built large hospitals and schools, which did much good, but they had failed to realize that economics and sociology were important. They were trapped 'by the fear that most of us surely have of revolution itself, of the Chinese masses taking initiative into their own hands'. The communists, meanwhile, had moved into the villages and market towns with a much larger number of volunteers, less training and equipment, but much closer to the people. 'Can a China missionary be free of the fear that what was true of China is still true of India and Africa?'

Africa is going through an incredible class turmoil, and it is anybody's guess where it will lead. Four distinct classes are in conflict. The largest is that of the subsistence farmers. Their lot has changed very little except that there has been an increase in their levels of expectation. Secondly, there are the masses of younger people with six to ten years of schooling who are still unable to earn a wage because of unemployment; they drift to the towns in alarming and explosive numbers. The third group are the graduates and secondary school leavers, for whom there are still many openings, but they know that the jobs at the top are likely to be held for a long time by the fourth group: the élite who came to office and power after independence.

Where, in all this turmoil, are the missionary leaders going to place their emphasis? If they continue to back the rural, conservative Church they may find themselves increasingly irrelevant in the mainstream of African life. Should missionaries be up with the new leaders and the new élite? And if they do move in these circles where will it place them if there is a really strong swing left? What are the African, Indian and Latin American churches going to do in the face of the massive move to the towns and the appalling urban poverty? The failure of the churches to come out on the issues of poverty in the Industrial Revolution of the West created a divorce between the ordinary man and the Church, from which the Church has never recovered. It looks very doubtful whether the Church can stay the pace with African and Asian urbanization any more than it did in the West.

*   *   *

Perhaps the worst problem facing missionary societies is the alarming fall off in recruitment in recent years. This is, of course, tied in to all the other problems. Part of the tail-off is connected with the theological revolution. Although Christians may emerge from their questionings as more tolerant human beings, this is not the myth quality that inspired so many of the earlier missionaries. In a way, the missionary has been the Protestant equivalent of the Catholic priest: representing a kind of saintliness beyond more normal mortal attainment. It is perhaps no accident that recruitment to the Catholic priesthood is going through the same crisis as recruitment to Protestant missions. This is not an age for myths and heroes. The Mill Hill Fathers, deliberating the problem say:

> The Church appears to many modern youths as part of the decadent institutions of an irrelevant and impersonal world, continuing practices from which they wish to be free. Secularisation and new concepts of authority and personal relationships, together with the effects of affluence, are felt before the Church herself has had time to absorb these ideas. To very many young people, celibacy, life-long commitment, special dress, strange living patterns and other forms of institutionalism seem incongruous. It has been said that 'before young people can commit themselves to the priesthood they must first know it and, secondly, admire it'. Modern youth hardly knows us and certainly finds it hard to admire us. Any remedy for the vocation crisis must include a renewed image of the missionary and, above all, a more effective communication between missionaries and modern youth.

We wonder if 'the vocation crisis' isn't deeper even than this. In all the young people we met going through training there was a consistent theme: they want to serve not preach. And they want to serve as 'ordinary people'. They were more scared of haloes than almost anything else. Christianity, for them, is a personal faith, a personal following of a Christ who is real to them. It is not, and probably can never be again, a didactic passing on of doctrines.

It is, we think, a healthy change in emphasis. And if the missionary societies were to blazen this new emphasis and be proud of it, one suspects they might find their recruiting problems evaporated. But this may be asking for too much; the matrix of missionary support is so complex, and some still want a Billy Graham style conquest of the world.

Of one thing we are sure: if young Christians in Britain saw the need in developing countries, if they saw the fun and the joy that goes with really meeting people of other countries, they would be glad to be counted with tomorrow's 'missionaries'.